Don't Take the Bait

A GUIDE TO HEALTHY CO-PARENTING AFTER DIVORCE

BY DOUGLAS CASE

Don't Take the Bait: A Guide to Healthy Co-Parenting After Divorce

Trilogy Christian Publishers A Wholly Owned Subsidiary of Trinity Broadcasting Network

2442 Michelle Drive Tustin, CA 92780

Copyright © 2022 by Douglas Case

Scripture quotations marked MSG are taken from THE MESSAGE, copyright © 1993, 2002, 2018 by Eugene H. Peterson. Used by permission of NavPress. All rights reserved. Represented by Tyndale House Publishers, Inc. Scripture quotations marked NIV are taken from the Holy Bible, New International Version®, NIV®. Copyright © 1973, 1978, 1984, 2011 by Biblica, Inc.TM Used by permission of Zondervan. All rights reserved worldwide. www.zondervan.com. The "NIV" and "New International Version" are trademarks registered in the United States Patent and Trademark Office by Biblica, Inc.TM Scripture quotations marked NLV are taken from the *New Life Version*, Copyright © 1969 and 2003. Used by permission of Barbour Publishing, Inc., Uhrichsville, Ohio 44683. All rights reserved.

No part of this book may be reproduced, stored in a retrieval system, or transmitted by any means without written permission from the author. All rights reserved. Printed in the USA.

Rights Department, 2442 Michelle Drive, Tustin, CA 92780.

Trilogy Christian Publishing/TBN and colophon are trademarks of Trinity Broadcasting Network.

For information about special discounts for bulk purchases, please contact Trilogy Christian Publishing.

Trilogy Disclaimer: The views and content expressed in this book are those of the author and may not necessarily reflect the views and doctrine of Trilogy Christian Publishing or the Trinity Broadcasting Network.

Manufactured in the United States of America

10 9 8 7 6 5 4 3 2 1

Library of Congress Cataloging-in-Publication Data is available.

ISBN: 979-8-88738-089-6

E-ISBN: 979-8-88738-090-2

Dedication

To my amazing wife, Laura Case. Without your support, love, and encouragement, I would not be able to accomplish all that God has planned for me. I am thankful for your warm heart and the love you show me endlessly. Also, to my five awesome, wild kids, you each challenge me to become a better person and father. You keep our lives full and interesting, and I cannot imagine it any other way.

And last but certainly not least, to my pastors, family, and friends that have encouraged me and challenged me in this journey. I appreciate the wisdom and grace you have given me, and it is my prayer that this book can do for others what you have done for me. I am deeply honored to be a part of all that God is doing at HighRidge Church! It is an honor to serve our awesome city of Longview.

I am forever grateful that Jesus saved me, chose me, and loves me.

Table of Contents

Introduction................................. 7

Chapter One: It's Over, Now What?.............. 17

Chapter Two: Five Words or Less................ 27

Chapter Three: Single Parent Focus.............. 45

Chapter Four: Next Round—Remarriage.......... 61

Chapter Five: Blending Families 87

Chapter Six: Fighting for Unity and Peace........ 107

Chapter Seven: Respecting Boundaries
and Trusting Authority...................... 123

Chapter Eight: New Kids, Who Dis?............. 149

Chapter Nine: It's Not Your Money 159

Chapter Ten: Changing Residence 171

Chapter Eleven: Changing Your Legacy
Through Forgiveness....................... 181

Appendix 191

Introduction

"We have five children; we are a blended family." That is how most of my conversations start. I meet someone new, and they ask me to tell them about my family. What I love most, though, is watching their face. I love seeing their reaction when I share those words with them. They look puzzled, shocked, or even surprised. They usually tilt their head and say something like "really" or "that's interesting."

The shocking part about this statement isn't that we have five kids. It usually is because they know my occupation; I am a pastor, and they are shocked to hear we have a blended family. If we are being real here, when it comes to the church, we don't always consider blended families, and we don't like addressing the issue of divorce. In most churches, we focus on telling people to work on their marriage, and even though I believe it is true, there are times when it is not possible. In addition, we don't always give parenting tips to people who adopt children or raise someone else's kids because of a previous marriage or relationship.

That surprises me because *the church is one big, blended family*. Please hear me, God has a plan for traditional families, and His way, of course, is the master design. He did not get this wrong, and He didn't intend for divorce; however, we have a God who can redeem and restore anything even when there is brokenness. There are biblical reasons for divorce, and I would never recommend it if you can reconcile; however, statistics show us this is a common trend in society and even the church.

When we think about pastors, we typically think about them serving and leading in church but not what they had to walk through. We are not much different than anyone else. Pastors have failures and shortfalls, and we know God can use anyone because He is using us, some of the most broken people in the world. Jeremiah 30:17 (NIV) states, *"'I will restore you to health and heal your wounds,' declares the Lord, 'because you are called an outcast, Zion for whom no one cares.'"* That verse speaks to me personally because, at those low moments, I felt like an outcast.

I felt that no one cared, but that wasn't the truth. In reality, the church and its leaders were the ones who stepped in and loved me, guided me, and helped me through my mistakes and my divorce. If you have had past hurts from church leaders, I apologize for them. I am sorry that some-

Introduction

one hurt you and might have pushed you away from what God intended to help, heal, and restore. But our God intended the church to do exactly what I just shared, to be a healthy place to recover, heal, and grow. In my brokenness, I had to turn from my past patterns of sin and repent. I needed to see that I had someone that cared. I served a God who wanted to restore me, and He placed people in my life to assist with the process.

I have an amazing wife with five kids; yes, we have five kids, as stated above, and I am remarried. God knew what He was doing. Our house is crazy at times! Each one of our kids has its own unique personality. Over the years, my wife and I both worked multiple jobs, served in the church, served our community, completed graduate courses, and had to alternate weekends where we were empty nesters.

What is most amazing is how we met and worked together to give our kids the best future possible for the circumstance they have to walk through. Is our life perfect? Of course not. Do our kids have past hurts and wounds? Of course, they do. But I fully believe in my heart that God is working on those daily. He is restoring what was broken, and He is responsible for fixing what we could not fix.

Years ago, I was walking through my divorce when I

decided to visit my pastor, Pastor Tim Ingram, and seek guidance. I wish I could say I was living a clean life, obeying God, and chasing after Him with all I had, but that was not the case. I just got out of the hospital and believed God was nudging me to visit my friend and pastor, Tim Ingram.

I was in the hospital because the stress of the divorce, being rejected from a prior spouse (I had my fair share in it as well), losing time with my daughter, etc., was so stressful that it almost gave me a stroke. The divorce was hard, and instead of seeking God, I was looking for approval. I just wanted to be wanted. While walking through the inevitable pain of divorce, I chose several wrong paths to numb the pain, one of which was internet dating. Not that meeting someone online is a problem; the problem was in my mind I was going to cross boundaries and approach it the wrong way. On top of all that, it was even dumber because my divorce wasn't even final at the time. I was still married, sleeping around now, and skipping time with my daughter. I would tell people I was alright, but in reality, I was in so much pain and very hurt.

I remember lying in the hospital bed, having my blood pressure the highest it ever has been, when I said out loud, "God, if You get me through this, I will do anything You ask." It was a dangerous prayer, but I meant it. I felt the

Introduction

Lord leading me to visit my friend Pastor Tim, who had recently moved to Longview, Texas, and to admit my mistakes to him and seek guidance on where to go from here. Let me help you with one of the best things I can give you; when you are in pain and need help, don't isolate yourself. Seek out someone who has walked through similar struggles and has the life that you want. They can help you avoid mistakes, make good choices, and can empathize with your pain. Three days later, I obeyed the Lord; I drove to Longview. During that time, I clearly heard the Lord give me direction for my life, that I would be a pastor, and that Longview would be my next home. None of these things were in my plan, but after the bold prayer I prayed in the hospital, I knew God was calling me to obedience and to a life that I always desired but didn't know how to get on my own. Not only had God spared my life, but He was also healing me physically, spiritually, emotionally, and mentally. I owed Him everything; at this point, obedience was the only option.

I repented to Pastor Tim and apologized for not taking his advice about walking in purity. I vividly remember telling him, "If God wants me to be married again, He's going to have to put her on a platform at church." I had no clue that God would do just that, and right after my conversation with Pastor Tim. Actually, it happened the *same day*!

That evening, walking into HighRidge Longview, I noticed a woman on the platform with a beautiful voice leading worship. I felt the Lord tell me, "That is your wife." I remember wrestling with that thought…thinking things like, "God, I am broken. I am not ready. I know I told You I would do anything, but this feels like a lot." I surrendered my will to God and introduced myself, and we had a quick conversation. This might sound romantic, but it was not. It was two surrendered, hurt, and broken individuals saying "yes" to what God had next. This is how most things work out for me; I am hesitant, I hear the Lord speak, nudging me to obey to take the next step of faith, and then hope for the best.

The next night as Laura and I were talking and getting to know each other, I shared my story with her. I shared the good, the bad, and the ugly. I told her we could only be friends until my divorce was finalized. We agreed to pray and fast before we made anything official. (The Bible discusses fasting over seventy times throughout the Word; it is important to God that we align ourselves spiritually with Him when we are making major decisions. Prayer and fasting together will help you hear God's will and align your heart with His plan. We decided to take this approach because we both knew that we couldn't walk through another divorce. We have faced that pain by doing it our way

Introduction

before, but this time we wanted to align with God's Word over our thoughts, fears, feelings, or hesitations.)

Wrapping up our conversation, I knew I had to say something that was hard to say, but obedience was easy at this point because I had done everything so wrong before. I was determined to get this one right; I told Laura that I would not sleep with her until we got married if marriage was what God had for us. She began crying, and I was confused why tears were rolling down her face. I was confident this was the right approach, but I didn't know why she was crying until she said to me, "That is everything I have been waiting to hear." She opened up, stating that it was a mistake she had made in her past marriage. She let her own beliefs and boundaries fall to the side before she married her first husband and wrestled with it after her divorce.

We ended up getting to know each other after we prayed and fasted and got married five months after the day we met. Again, it was obedience for both of us; if you saw my awful haircut, you would understand why she was being obedient. I joke with her to this day that it was my single mom lifestyle, but in reality, I needed some help. We have been married for five of the best years of my life, and I never imagined God could orchestrate a better story than ours, even though it has had its challenges.

We have been co-parenting with our first spouses, and I hope this book will help those who have been in similar situations. No parent wants their kids to come from a non-traditional/broken home; however, there are times it just has to happen. The Bible is very clear on those times, but it is also clear on grace, forgiveness, and having plans for you.

It doesn't matter what your story is; God wants to use you to impact and leave a legacy. In divorce, both parties have contributed. It doesn't matter who you point the finger at if you aren't willing to reflect and see how you contributed to the end result. That is how we learn, by looking inward and seeing what areas we need to grow in so that we can flourish.

My goal for writing this book is to give you tools and values that were taught, passed on, or instilled in me to ensure that I could co-parent well and see my kids flourish. My overall goal is to share these resources with you and see them impacting your kids and their future. We have to value marriage, but we also need to see there are ways to co-parent when restoration isn't possible. As you read this book, you will see I didn't have it all together. Actually, I was a hot mess trying to figure it out. I hope you can learn from my mistakes and avoid having to walk through the

Introduction

same things I share in my story. Last of all, please know this, I still don't have it all together. I still make plenty of mistakes, say dumb things, and can get defensive about my point of view. My hope is that being open and transparent in my mistakes will help you navigate your own journey.

Overall, I know that kids are resilient. They dream big, bounce back, and can recover faster than us adults. Even if you have made mistakes in the past, remember it is never too late to change course, own your part in it, and adjust. Watch what God can do when you take faith steps towards Him! God can use your mess and turn it into a beautiful thing.

CHAPTER ONE:

It's Over, Now What?

I remember sitting on the floor in my parents' house. The bathroom was not very big, especially for a guy my size. I am about six feet, four inches, and 260 pounds, but this bathroom was maybe four by six feet, including the shower and the sink that took up most of it. I was squeezed in between the sink and the wall, using them as a brace to hold me upright. I was crying. Actually, I was sobbing with two doors locked so my senior citizen parents couldn't come in and hear me. It was one of those ugly cries that, as a man, we pretend never happened. The type where we are almost hyperventilating and snot is pouring out. It pains me to even share that to this day, but there are times we have all been there.

It was at that moment I had a reality check. I realized right then that I was done with the long fights, wondering how this would change, and finally looking ahead. I realized that my daughter was the only thing that mattered to me. I realized how angry I was for everyone who lied to me, gave me false hope, or wanted me to believe the best about the situation. I was a ball of emotions, and they came flooding in all at once. I also realized I was hurt, in pain, and couldn't imagine what the future would look like. I didn't plan for divorce; I never even thought of it for the first nine years of my marriage.

I was married for eleven years, and for the longest time, I really believed we would not be a statistic. I thought my marriage could handle anything. I believed because our parents had been married for so long, we would never reach a divorce. We had been through a lot, mostly bad decisions, but I thought a few months before the moment balling in the bathroom, the storm had passed. I was wrong, and even though we were getting divorced, I knew I could survive it if I relied on God, but I didn't trust Him. I didn't understand why all the prayers weren't answered and why I had to walk through all of this. I didn't know He had a better plan and would work it out before I could even see it.

In all this, the thing that hit me the hardest, though, was that my daughter wouldn't be with me daily anymore. This was gut-wrenching. She was my world, and I loved her. We wouldn't have daily conversations on the way to school, days in the park wasting the afternoon, and our household would be split. It made me angry, upset, and wanting to have control over the situation.

This is where I would tell you to stop there. Don't make phone calls, text, or listen to yourself at this moment. Call a friend that can give you sound wisdom, pray, go to church, do anything except pick up that phone and try to discuss it. You are not stable enough when this reality hits you to make sound decisions. Maybe I am the only one who makes bad decisions when I am emotional, but I highly doubt that.

This is where I hit rock bottom. I remember calling my daughter's mom and starting one of the worse negotiations in the world. I tried to use guilt, shame, and bribery. None of it worked, and I am glad it didn't.

I started the phone conversation with, "I want to discuss Aubrey." I remember her mom stating, "There isn't anything to discuss. We can be civil, and we will work at sharing time between us." I then followed up by pointing only blame on her. I am sure making my daughter's mom feel bad and bullied didn't help my case and open her up to new suggestions. I then stated, "I will give you anything we have if you don't take her from me."

Don't Take the Bait

I was acting like a child fighting over a possession. I was brokering the deal like it was a used car. I was being the pushy salesman trying to get the upper hand in the deal. I wish this wasn't the story. I wish I could say I knew right away that I was going to be okay and my daughter would be fine, but I didn't.

I wish I would have grabbed Jeremiah 29:11 and spoken over myself that the Lord had plans for me. Plans to prosper! Unfortunately, it felt like God was nowhere close. It's funny what an amazing Father we have because He doesn't save us in our pain all the time. Sometimes He uses it as one of the best lessons we have ever received. He allows it because He can see ahead and how this moment will change your life.

If not for this moment, I am not sure I would be on the path I am now. I don't know if I would have repented, chased after the Lord, or been obedient to share any of this with you. I believe God puts purpose to our pain; He works all things together for His good. He also has shown me many times it isn't all about me anyways. He has a sense of humor in all of it because He knows there is something better for you if you turn back to Him, but He won't force it. He is that loving!

I realized right at that moment, as I begged, pleaded,

and gave my best sales pitch, that I had nothing left. My daughter was really my idol and was more important than my relationship with God. I realized that I was trying to write my daughter's mom out of my daughter's life. I was so bitter that I only wanted my daughter to be with me and show everyone else I was the "good guy" in this story.

The truth of the matter is a child shouldn't have to pick sides. There isn't a winner and loser in this situation, but I see it time and time again when people separate and divorce; they want to win at all costs. They overlook that there is a child in the middle who lost their entire world and two adults who are the only ones who had any say in it. That is exactly what I did as well. The end game should be creating an environment where your kids feel loved by both parents no matter what has happened in the past. This needs to be done with boundaries, grace, and following authority and your decree.

At the time of the discussion, I was not in a healthy place. I was in the "forget you" stage of my divorce. I put all the blame on my ex-wife and took none of the responsibility. I didn't recognize that my prior decisions didn't create a place for a thriving marriage. I wasn't all to blame, but I didn't establish a godly marriage. I had major pain from my childhood, pornography addiction, and lust after different women as a married man. I didn't make my wife feel secure. *"For you may be sure of this, that everyone who is sexually immoral or impure, or who is covetous (that is, an idolater), has no inheritance in the kingdom of Christ and God"* (Ephesians 5:5, ESV).

To start with a healthy relationship, we have to lead as men with purity. This is something that became very clear to me when I was lying in the hospital bed. I needed to change, and I needed to date the right way and build a marriage as God intended if I wanted to set an example for my daughter. I wanted my ceiling to be my daughter's floor, meaning I wanted her to have an advantage of broken strongholds before it was too late.

I also realized then that I didn't live my life for my wife. We had problems for years, and while we struggled, I would pull closer and closer to my daughter. I thought that if I focused on being a dad and appeared to have it together, then it would work itself out.

I would stress to any parent reading this book or debating separate households to fight for your marriage at all costs. But if there are biblical grounds for divorce, make sure you stay close to people who will challenge you to walk with the Lord, dig in His Word, and stay under spiritual authority. No one wants to be challenged in this situation; we want to be validated. However, going back to spiritual authority saved me from making more mistakes. I walked away from the wisdom in the past, and I knew God was leading me back to it.

The steps, challenges, and mistakes discussed in each chapter remaining in this book personally helped me grow and get closer to the Lord. There were times family, friends, and coworkers weren't supportive or didn't understand what I was going through, and that's okay. They were keys to creating an environment for healthy co-parenting, raising step kids, building a biblical marriage after divorce, and getting healing. God even used my mistakes to bring me closer to Him; He will do the same for you if you allow Him to address them.

My hope is that no one would ever walk through a divorce; however, the statistics do not show that. In the U. S., there is a divorce every thirteen seconds. The average first marriage lasts about eight years. This was never God's intent, but it is a reality of our sin and brokenness. Most people get remarried within three years after divorce, and co-parenting can be a major hurdle when blending a family. We have a huge divorce rate in this day and age and a second marriage divorce rate that I do not think God ever intended with His plan. The best part, though, is we serve a God that is all about restoration. He is all about His children. He is a God of second and third chances; it is up to us if we follow it.

The goal of this book, though, is to help those who have walked through a divorce with kids, those who want to remarry with kids, and those who want to provide their kids with the best gift they can—a healthy remarriage with great co-parenting at two households.

Let me reiterate that I am currently walking this journey with you. I don't have all the answers, and Laura and I are constantly navigating through blending our family, getting healing from our past, and being obedient to what God has for us. We have been together only five years, I don't have all the answers, but luckily, I have people around me that have shared wisdom I believe needs to be shared with others.

Blending families is hard. It's like raising kids, each one is different, and they need to be approached in different ways. There isn't a manual to walk you through the process. But we have to start someplace. We have to start sharing our experiences and stories so that we can create a better future for families. I hope this book encourages you to share your journey as well. To share the mistakes you made, the challenges you faced, and to share decisions the Holy Spirit guided you to.

Chapter Reflection

Holy Spirit, what are You saying to me?

_____
_____
_____
_____
_____
_____
_____
_____
_____
_____
_____
_____
_____
_____
_____
_____
_____
_____

CHAPTER TWO:

Five Words or Less

It was an awesome day at the river with my entire family in Pennsylvania. We were visiting during summer from Texas, where the heat is unbearable, and enjoying the seventy-six-degree sunshine. The sun was hot, the water was cold, and I was there with my future wife—granted, this was 2017. We were engaged and waiting to get married after dating a short time; we will discuss this in a later chapter.

We decided to visit my hometown to see my family and give my future wife and her kids a tour of where I grew up, share family stories, and show them what life was like in the Northeast. My wife is a native Texan who had never visited Pennsylvania, let alone planned to marry a Yankee. We were loading up and getting ready to get dinner when a text popped up on my phone from my ex-wife. My first thought was, *Oh, man. What now? I am sure she is mad about something, and I know she isn't thrilled that*

I am getting married, my daughter was quick to share as soon as we got engaged.

I was wrong. The text was actually something I didn't expect or even think would happen. My ex-wife sent a message asking for forgiveness. She asked me to forgive the mistakes she made, the hurt she caused, and the choices she made. I remember reading it to my soon-to-be wife and thought, *What is going on?* I text back something similar to "I forgive you. I never held it against you, and I hope you do well. I want us to be able to make great decisions for our daughter. Have a great day."

I then called my pastor and told him about the text and how I responded and asked, "What do you recommend?" The situation to that point was not good between my ex-wife and me. We still had a lot of anger, worried about our daughter and how she was doing, and just got through discussing my engagement to my soon-to-be wife.

Not everyone will have their pastor as their accountability person; I was grateful mine was a close friend who had been through similar situations. You just need to have someone that you can be honest with and share the struggles and wins with them. It can be a close friend, a group leader, or even a boss. Don't put limitations on relationships; find the person who God put in your life to have accountability with. My only advice, though, is that they push you closer to your relationship with the Lord, not validate your feelings or pat you on the back. If they get you stirred up and want to react, that person probably isn't a great accountability partner.

I still laugh, thinking back to what my pastor said to me when I read the message. He just said, "I wouldn't have texted that!" I was thinking to myself, *What are you talking about? I am trying to make the right decisions and find some peace for my daughter. I was saying I forgive her. I was working on trying to encourage a good healthy co-parenting relationship.* I sat on the phone waiting for him to add, but he was quiet, he is a great communicator, and one of the things I love about him is he will let awkward silence sit. I am not that way, so I was trying to explain myself. The more I said, the quieter he got; it was like he slowed his breathing down even. I was trying to tell him I did the right thing, but he just remained silent. I finally asked him, "What should I have said?"

This was when Pastor Tim Ingram shared the most brilliant thing I have ever heard. He stated, "When you talk too much or text a lot back, it doesn't leave room for the Holy Spirit. You end up taking the credit and getting in the way. With all the battles you have had, and with all the progress you have made in trusting the Lord, you need to speak less. I wouldn't ever respond with more than five words. If it can't be addressed in five words or less, then wait. As time passes, you will know what you can and can't say, but for now, a good rule of thumb is five words or less, and it can't be rude. Just answer what is being asked or ignore it. There is nothing wrong with pausing." Jesus says in Scripture says, *"But the Advocate, the Holy Spirit, whom the Father will send in my name, will teach you all things and will remind you of everything I have said to you"* (John 14:26, NIV).

This verse reminded me that I need the Holy Spirit to be my advocate. The Holy Spirit is a gift from God, and instead of making it weird (something man does, not God), we can rely on Him to say what we need to say.

I had an extremely hard time implementing this advice, though. I remember thinking, *How do you ever say anything in five words or less?* I talk all the time! Even when I was writing this book, I thought, *Man, my words come out way faster than I can even type.* When I was navigating the beginning stages of co-parenting, the Holy Spirit brought so many scriptures to my mind about speaking less and listening more. These scriptures included:

"Know this, my beloved brothers: let every person be

quick to hear, slow to speak, slow to anger; for the anger of man does not produce the righteousness of God" (James 1:19–20, ESV).

"Even a fool who keeps silent is considered wise; when he closes his lips, he is deemed intelligent" (Proverbs 17:28, ESV).

"Whoever keeps his mouth and his tongue keeps himself out of trouble" (Proverbs 21:23, ESV).

I believe, a lot of times, when we are trying to co-parent, we end up speaking way too much. We try to have answers for everything, justify our actions, and then get emotional about how wrong the other parent can be. I remember thinking about all kinds of things that I wanted to share. I wanted to discuss what I approved of and what I didn't with my ex-wife in regard to her approach. I am positive she could say the same. At this point, I was quick to argue, throw the past in her face, and constantly remind her of all the wrong she had done. Heaping shame and guilt onto the other person never has and never will be a part of forwarding progress.

But when a text would come in, or a disagreement would occur, I would shut up after receiving the advice I got from Pastor Tim. If I wanted to reply, I would open a new text and start writing. I cannot tell you how many times I would get angry and frustrated when I would count my words and see, "Man, I have six or seven words." Again, if it can't be said in five or less, it probably doesn't need to be addressed then.

How Long Do I Do This?

A question that is often asked from friends who have walked this road is, how long do I need to apply this "five words or less" to our co-parenting relationship? You need to do this till there is peace and you can work together. If there is conflict, then you go back to this approach. Another piece of advice given to me was to stick to your divorce decree or custody agreement. Legal protection and covering are there for a purpose; this can protect us even from ourselves. You agreed to it, so stick with what you agreed to. If there are changes needed, they can happen in peaceful conversations in time.

In reality, this took us about a year before the arguments and disagreements fully stopped. I had to watch every word I said because I was remarried during this time. During this year, I had to bring my now wife, Laura, in on these conversations to make sure I wasn't cold or harsh or crossing any boundaries. It was important to me that Laura and I remained on the same page. I now had to think about my wife, my daughter, and our children when I made changes or decisions regarding our family. I would be very careful about how to reply to a text. As the year passed, I would ask my wife for help making sure I wasn't staying cold but also not crossing any boundaries in my communication. I wanted to make sure we were on the same page since I was remarried, and it affected my wife, not just my daughter, when I had to make changes or decisions regarding our family.

As of now, my ex-wife and I can discuss switching weekends, my daughter's needs, discipline, etc., because we spoke less and let the heated discussions and arguments pass. We have stuck to the decree for the most part but will give extra time to the other parent when there are big events, family trips, or vacations. It has worked out well because I learned when to shut up.

Again, this is easier for me to write than it was for me to walk through, but you can do it; it can be done. It took months of forming a new habit in my own life when I wanted to say way more than five words. I often fought the urge to try and control the situation, say something harsh or correct my ex, but this hadn't worked out well in the past, so I was determined to try this new way.

Stick to the Decree

When we make the decision to honor God and honor the other person by speaking less and creating healthy boundaries, it makes it easier to focus on whatever legal agreement you have both agreed to. It may not look exactly how you want it to, but it never does. No one gets the perfect decree or legal agreement when it comes to their children or divorce. In our initial decree, it was pretty fair, 50/50 time with our daughter. However, God once again asked me to trust His plan. This required a big job change and a move. I knew there were parts of our decree that I didn't like; they didn't fit into my life and would require a lot more time and energy.

I know what you are thinking; I don't like the decree, and it doesn't have what I want in it. Guess what? No one ever gets the perfect decree or legal agreement when it comes to their kids. In my initial decree, it was pretty fair, and time was split down the middle; however, as life changed, I got called into ministry, which required me to move. I saw there were things in my new decree that flat out didn't work for me and what I wanted to do, including driving.

I knew God was calling me from Central Texas to East Texas. I fought it tooth and nail, but God does that at times.

Five Words or Less

He will put something in your heart you can't say no to. I remember thinking to myself, *I finally have some stability, I have a house here, I have my job here; God, do You know what You are doing? I'm not sure about this East Texas thing, but I am going to trust You.* With moving, I knew I would have to discuss the changes with my ex-wife, get an attorney, and create a new decree.

The conversation didn't go well with my ex-wife because it felt like I was changing my mind after we agreed to the original decree, and she was right; I was. The cost of another attorney always causes issues in our minds, at least for me. I hate paying for attorney bills, and my divorce left a bad taste in my mouth of how expensive our legal system can be. Last of all, I knew I would have to make one of the hardest decisions of my life. I would only get my daughter going forward on weekends and summers. This was painful, but I knew God had a plan, and I needed to be obedient.

We reached an agreement after about a month, and it required a few things of me. I would pay support, provide insurance, and drive the three hours each way for pick up and drop off. This means that every other weekend, I would spend almost twelve hours in the car. I remember being really upset about it, and God nudged me to agree to it, don't complain, and follow authority.

I spent lots of time in prayer, asking God if this was really His way. I would kneel down in my closet without distractions and tell Him I was staying put till I heard His voice. God would comfort me, guide me, and push me to accept His will over my own plans. I would discuss the agreement with my spiritual authority, and they would agree with it, confirming again this is what God had for me. Last of all, I would spend time in the Word, and God would point out scriptures telling me to trust Him. Getting practical meant that I put my focus on God and what He was saying over what the new agreement had in it.

The decree or legal agreement you finalize is legal authority, and we hate authority in America! No one likes to be told, "This is what you are going to do, and there are no exceptions." We need to, in those times, remember that God has blessings for those who fall under authority. I am constantly reminded of the centurion in the Bible who knew authority. Since he understood it, was under it, and followed it, he was seen as a man of big faith. I want the same for my life—to be seen as a man of big faith. Let's take a look at Matthew, where Jesus recognized obeying authority as big faith.

Five Words or Less

When Jesus had entered Capernaum, a centurion came to him, asking for help. "Lord," he said, "my servant lies at home paralyzed, suffering terribly." Jesus said to him, "Shall I come and heal him?" The centurion replied, "Lord, I do not deserve to have you come under my roof. But just say the word, and my servant will be healed. For I myself am a man under authority, with soldiers under me. I tell this one, 'Go,' and he goes; and that one, 'Come,' and he comes. I say to my servant, 'Do this,' and he does it." When Jesus heard this, he was amazed and said to those following him, "Truly I tell you, I have not found anyone in Israel with such great faith. I say to you that many will come from the east and the west, and will take their places at the feast with Abraham, Isaac and Jacob in the kingdom of heaven. But the subjects of the kingdom will be thrown outside, into the darkness, where there will be weeping and gnashing of teeth." Then Jesus said to the centurion, "Go! Let it be done just as you believed it would." And his servant was healed at that moment.

Matthew 8:5–13 (NIV)

Because of his faith and trust in authority, God healed the servant. I believe we see some of God's biggest blessings when we submit and humble ourselves. We may not like it, we may not agree with it, but there is a blessing to being under authority.

As I started driving every other weekend for about twelve hours in the car, my attitude at first was not good. Actually, it was horrible. I was angry, and my back hurt. I was tired when I got home and would think about how I only had a day and a half with my daughter at my house. It wasn't enough time for only seeing her every other weekend, and I really wanted more. I remember being upset at the price of gas and how I would need to buy food and eat while driving (something I personally don't like). On top of that, I hated sitting in rush hour traffic on a Friday afternoon in Dallas, Irving, and Fort Worth. It drove me nuts! I am not patient, and traffic is the one pet peeve I didn't have healing yet. I think I am still working on it. Last of all, the mileage I was putting on my truck was driving me insane. I thought to myself, *This truck will be ruined in three years, then what do I do?*

As a few months passed, I submitted to it. I found some amazing blessings in the drive that, at first, I overlooked. I found a place where I could listen to sermons and books as I drove, have the Bible app read scripture to me, and sometimes sit quietly and listen to the Lord. On rides with my daughter, we had intentional uninterrupted time to talk about her week and dreams, watch a show and laugh. I had more direct time with her being in that car than you get with a busy teenager's schedule when they have school, sports, and friends.

God gave me quality time with my daughter, and even though gas, wear and tear on my vehicle, and eating out cost me, it was nothing to the closeness I got with her.

I was driving every other week, and my attitude toward it changed. I remember telling God while praying that if I do this for the next few years, it will build in extra prayer time and time with my daughter, and I am learning a lot for ministry. I thanked God for having me submit to something that wasn't always fun or pleasant but caused growth. During this time of driving back and forth, I wasn't full-time in ministry yet but knew there was a day coming when I would be. I decided I was going to take advantage of the ride by listening to podcasts, books, sermons, etc., to grow and get ready for what God had next.

On top of building a great relationship with my daughter driving in those times, one day, God wanted to show off. He had something way better planned, and because of the good/lucky choices I made to drive, He spoke very clearly to me. I remembered listening to a John Maxwell discussion he had at Church of the Highlands. The message was very simple, which is good for me, and it discussed if you want to change the world, then serve someone daily. It is a simple process we can take and, over time, will impact many. It creates a ripple effect when we serve someone well.

I am a huge John Maxwell fan! I mean, when I got the Maxwell Leadership Bible, I read it cover to cover in less than six months. His application of the Word to business situations and leadership spoke to me since I have a background in business and degrees in it. I remember saying out loud to myself, "What person could I serve tomorrow?" I decided I would start tonight and see if my wife needed anything. I called, and she asked for food from Whataburger. I was thrilled because who doesn't love Whataburger? As I hung up the phone, I had a crazy thought. I thought about what it would be like to have time to sit with John Maxwell and ask him some questions. He is the businessman version of Billy Graham. Very clearly, I heard the Lord say to me, "Why don't you invite him?"

I was driving down the highway thinking, *Doug, that is crazy.* Again, I heard, not audible, but in my head, "Why don't you invite him?" I rushed to pull up his website and found the email to request John to speak at an event. As I browsed the website, I told myself, *This is not possible.* I started to debate how can I ever bring someone like that to the city I live in. I love Longview, but there is no way I could ever have the finances, credibly, let alone a commitment from John to attend. I decided that I would send the link to my own email and would address it later. I never said a word when I got home and ate with my wife.

That night as I was sleeping, I had a dream that John Maxwell flew into our city to speak at the event I was hosting. I woke up three times thinking to myself, *I need to email and request him to come.* The next morning, I couldn't shake the thought. I rushed the kids to school, got home, pulled out my laptop, and drafted the email stating that I would love a conference where we would bring church, business, and community leaders together to work on the issues facing our area. That if John could come, he could encourage and challenge our leaders to serve those around them and change our city one person at a time. My hope was the community would build momentum, and if we invested in the leaders, it would last for generations. I sent the email and didn't tell anyone, first because I still couldn't believe I sent it, and second because it seemed insane.

That day my wife came home from lunch with a friend who got a job offer from Dr. John Townsend. She was so excited because she could work for someone she really admired. My wife asked me if I ever thought of becoming a John Maxwell coach.

I was puzzled, wondering where this conversation was coming from; I didn't tell anyone about the email, so why now? The Holy Spirit was definitely speaking to both of us, and she said, "I want you to be able to meet John Maxwell. You really love his work, and this is a way you can have time to sit and ask some leadership questions." My response was, "No. I am not interested at all." I paused and continued with, "I am going to meet him because I am going to bring him to Longview." She asked what I was talking about, and I explained the email. What I love most about my wife is that she believed in me, she believed that I could do it, and she supported what I really felt God put on my heart.

Fast forward almost six months past that talk, and John Maxwell was in Longview, Texas, talking about community transformation. He was blown away by the amazing pastors we have in our city that decided to partner behind this idea and move it forward way past what I ever imagined it would be. He was impressed that we were the first to discuss what he planned as his legacy, and it made him agree to visit. We then started a partnership and became one of the pilot program cities to take this approach. Partnering with his organization has been such a blessing, and it all started because of a few hours in the car every other week.

In addition, John Bevere came to speak as well. He was excited about what we were doing, how the city was alive, and that we had pastors actually partnering with the city to make a difference. It was the cherry on top of the evening because I was such a big fan of John Bevere as well. God opened doors I never thought were possible, and it all came from a simple car ride and time with Him.

When we say yes to what God asks, even if we don't like it or understand it, we will see the benefits of being near to Him. I get to work with people now that I look up to. God had a plan in my life, but it could have been missed if I argued why I shouldn't drive or fought His calling to my amazing city! I am thankful daily for how God uses the smallest details to change our path. He allows me now to work with pastors, business owners, and city leaders to impact East Texas. I am excited about what He is going to do next in our area.

Chapter Reflection

Holy Spirit, what are You saying to me?

CHAPTER THREE:

Single Parent Focus

Being a single parent was one of the strangest times of my life. There were times in my first marriage before the divorce when I thought everything relied on me; however, her mom was still there for our daughter. I probably victimized this more than I should have in my first marriage, but once the divorce hit, it was very different. All of a sudden, I was responsible for everything; there was no asking, "Hey, can you grab this?" "Can you pick me up at this time?" "Can you adjust your schedule?" because there is no more partnership once we separated and filed.

When I reflected back on my first marriage, I realized that I built a lot of expectations on the one thing I could control. I pressured my daughter to achieve, earn my love, and perform. I became driven by her success because I was really failing everywhere else. I couldn't save my marriage, so I put her first, which was a big mistake. I think that would have continued and crushed her if it wasn't for the divorce. Every relationship fails when God is not at the center of it. The Bible states, *"Fathers, do not exasperate your children; instead, bring them up in the ...instruction of the Lord"* (Ephesians 6:4, NIV).

The hardest part for me was finding balance when my daughter was home and I had to work compared to when she wasn't, and I didn't want to come home and be by myself. When my daughter was with me, I struggled with the guilt and shame of divorce; I would blame myself for shaking her foundation and making her walk through this pain. I really started to reflect, and the Lord really helped me become softer. By loving the Lord deeper in this journey, everything else pretty much was gone or failed, which allowed me to reevaluate the type of father I was being.

I believe there are five different types of fathers. Mark Driscoll has discussed these at some point in his sermon series as well. They are:

Distant father—the father who abandoned you, passed away, or never took care of you.

Abusive father—someone that mistreats you, takes advantage of you, or physically, emotionally, or verbally abuses you. They treat you like you are a burden.

Strict father—you were raised that it was your responsibility to take care of yourself, rules were law, and you needed to work constantly to gain approval. It felt like a performance-based relationship. You never felt good enough or that your father was proud of you.

Emasculating father—a weak father who doesn't stand for anything. He is well-liked but not respected. Someone you wouldn't want to follow because he doesn't lead his family well.

Good father—loves the lord, leads his family well, is not toxic or pushes toxic masculinity, and loves to serve his family while protecting them.

Before my divorce, I was definitely the strict father. I was hard on my daughter, and I expected her to reach expectations that were unclear and unspoken and gave little room for failure. I was so hard on her because I was hard on myself. I regretted not taking my family to church soon enough, thinking I had it figured out, and not leading in a biblical way. During my first marriage, I drank a lot, became an addict to prescription pain pills, addicted to pornography, and really dove into depression. I was driven, but my focus was on everything besides the Lord. The divorce was the final straw in breaking me and trying to do it my way.

Don't Take the Bait

I remember one day, I was riding in the car with my daughter and feeling like the Lord was starting to heal me through the process. I was signing and goofing off with her in the car, and she was staring at me.

I asked her if everything was okay, and she bounced the question right back at me. Actually, she threw it right back on me! I was thinking to myself, *Of course, I am okay. I know it has been challenging, but I am in a good place.* I was seeing a counselor, in a small group serving at church, and even though the divorce was hard, I was on my way to moving forward. I remember asking her why she asked me that, and she stated, "Dad, I don't think I have ever seen you like this. I haven't ever seen you listen to music and sing. It just seems different; you usually are more serious."

This was crushing to me because I realized my joy was gone for so long. Before the brokenness, I was not relying on the Lord for my joy; I was relying on my situation. The Bible states,

> Consider it pure joy, my brothers and sisters, whenever you face trials of many kinds, because you know that the testing of your faith produces perseverance. Let perseverance finish its work so that you may be mature and complete, not lacking anything.
>
> **James 1:2–4 (NIV)**

Single Parent Focus

In my past, everything was a challenge, and I was ruled by my circumstances. It would throw me off when things didn't go right, it made me want to fix everything, and it gave no room for the Holy Spirit to correct me. This left no room for joy. There is a difference between joy and happiness. I wasn't happy that I was walking through a divorce, being a single parent, and trying to get help, but joy is deeper; it comes from your heart. *"The joy of the Lord is your strength"* (Nehemiah 8:10, NIV).

Without the Lord being my strength, joy was lacking. When joy was lacking, I got more and more controlling on the one thing I could influence, and that was how my daughter acted and behaved.

I realized I put so much pressure on her to meet my expectations that I had to own my part, and it was the first time the Lord told me to apologize. Growing up in my generation, parents didn't apologize to us if they got stuff wrong. We just were taught to listen and obey. I hate to admit it, but I never apologized to my daughter before that day. I never looked at her and said, "I am sorry for my part, I am sorry that I hurt you, and I will work on being better." I never took ownership of mistakes that I made; instead, I justified them by stating that I was the authority/parent.

I knew that repentance and becoming a good father

were more important than just the appearance of having it all together. A good father can admit when he has made mistakes, he can repent, and he can change. I told Aubrey that I was sorry for how hard I was on her all these years. I explained that it wasn't fair that I put pressure and unobtainable expectations on her to meet my needs. I told her I was going to work on myself more and try to be the best dad she could have. I knew I wouldn't get it perfect, but it was a defining moment that changed me.

If you have been in this situation or had a parent like this, I would like to start by saying I am sorry. They may not have known the impact they left. They may not know the damage they have done. They could have been doing what they were raised to do; however, that is not an excuse. You need to hear it just like my daughter needed to hear it—I am sorry. I am sorry that you had to walk through your challenges as well, and if you can accept that apology on behalf of your parent, I am sure the Lord will work on you becoming an amazing father or mother as well.

As time passed, I really worked on being patient. I prayed for God to help me with my anger, my selfish ambition, and most of all, my bitterness. It was a process, but this allowed me to start focusing on my daughter's needs rather than just what I expected. I became more relational with her and asked her about her thoughts and opinions rather than just telling her mine. This resulted in deep conversations about faith and what I was growing in, and it showed my daughter that my faith was growing more and more.

During the first year of separation, it was different because when she was with me, I had to be the dad and mom. My wife and I, in the first year, had to live apart week on week off since I needed to adjust my decree. Being a mom and dad at the same time was way outside my comfort zone.

I am not a very affectionate person, and I don't really use words of affirmation well. My daughter needed those more at that time than anything else. It was going to take a miracle to become that person she needed, especially when I was so hurt.

During that first year, my daughter actually showed me how to be a better Christian because she has a servant leader's heart. Let me explain that even more; my love languages are acts of service and quality time. My daughter would take care of things for me that, in the past, I overlooked.

She would ask me to watch a show, do a shared activity, or even just go for a ride on the motorcycle. She would get me a drink or grab something for me so that I wouldn't have to get up. Growing up, I was raised to respect my parents and the adults in the room. If they needed something, you got it out of obligation, not because you wanted to serve them. Aubrey didn't do it because I told her; she did it because she was growing her relationship with the Lord as well and chose to serve and love me the way I needed to be loved.

I decided I would pray that the Lord would rearrange my priorities and change how I interact with my daughter. I made a predetermined decision that would focus on being the best parent since she wouldn't see her mom during the week and not see her dad the following week. I knew that I needed to hug her, tell her I was proud of her, and speak life to her. It changed how I interacted in all my relationships.

In the weeks she wasn't with me, I focused on doing things to improve my health and really focused on spiritual health—something that was lacking for so long. When she was with me and went to bed, I read my Bible, listened to worship, and prayed. I prayed a lot to get through this time, and if you are reading this, I am sure you are too. Scripture tells us, "If you love me, keep my commands"

(John 14:15, NIV). As I dove into my spiritual health and read the Word, this area really stuck out for me. During the finalization of my divorce, I was in Freedom group. Pastor Chris Hodges read this and was discussing how many hear it. We have pain and can hear it in many ways, and what I read in that verse didn't sit well with me. The way I read the verse was God was angry and just telling me to do what He said. I could hear my own voice in it with the way I treated my daughter in the past. I felt disappointment inside my heart, thinking, *I can never do everything God demands.* Pastor Chris then went on to explain the simplest concept that I had overlooked for my entire life.

Pastor Chris explained that God isn't worried about the second part. He knows you will want to keep His commands if you just love Jesus. If we love Jesus, He will guide us and lead us to our Father's will. God has a much better plan for you. He is relational, He is intentional, and He is sovereign.

To find the balance of being a single parent, I needed the help of the Father, and I needed His guidance. The only way for me to clearly hear that was to love Jesus. You might be thinking the same thing I did that day, *How do we love Jesus?*

We love Jesus the same way we treat any relationship.

We have to get in His Word. I had to start reading my Bible and actually asking the Lord to speak to me through it. I started praying throughout the day, and it was as simple as a conversation with Him. I realized Jesus needed to be my best friend, and by doing that, I would have balance in being a single parent. I would have grace when I messed up, forgiveness when I overreacted, and most importantly, guidance on how to grow and be the best parent I could be for my daughter.

While praying over this, the Lord showed me some very clear things. He showed me some mistakes I made with control and how to fix it. I really had to realize that I had to give up control when my daughter was not in my house. I didn't have authority in my ex-wife's house, and I didn't want her to have it in mine. That doesn't mean we can't have discussions about our concerns relating to our daughter and work on agreements for raising her. What it does mean, though, is that I can't ultimately tell her what to do when my daughter is with her.

During the divorce process, I really didn't want random people in my daughter's life. So, I did what I normally do; I tried to control it. I told my soon-to-be ex-wife during the process that I was going to put a six-month waiting period before anyone could be introduced to our daughter. I thought, *If she can't introduce my daughter to them, then it will save her pain and keep another person out of parenting my kid.* I also had a lot of past trauma in my childhood, so I was very overprotective and thought of the worst-case scenarios.

I thought, *What if the person she brings home abuses my daughter? What if they are a creep? Or even worse, what if they make my daughter walk through the same trauma I faced being molested as a kid?* These fears were there, but God kept asking me, "Do you trust Me?" By the time we got to the lawyer's office, I decided not to include it.

At the time, I had a friend who had this in his decree. I thought it was a good idea until I saw him constantly lie about the timeframes, date random women, and wait just to the date to share they will be around his kids, and it was a mess. I decided that if we can manipulate it, we will, so why even include it? I need to just trust that God has it.

I'm glad I didn't put timeframes on it because I met my wife two weeks before we finalized the divorce. We agreed only to be friends and not date or do anything physical because my divorce wasn't finalized. I will go into that more in the next chapter. But the requirement would have probably changed our future, and I am thankful I gave up controlling it.

Don't Take the Bait

We have a saying at our church that we remind each other often, "choices lead and feelings follow." I believe we took this from Pastor Chris Hodges at Church of the Highlands; nothing is new under the sun. What we are saying, though, is that feelings are terrible leaders. They make you react and drive out of emotion rather than relying on truth. We have to make predetermined decisions to make choices that are based on Scripture/truth. Over time our feelings will line up.

I decided to make a decision that day. I am responsible for my household and no one else. I was reading my Bible during that time, and Joshua 24:15 stood out.

> But if serving the Lord seems undesirable to you, then choose for yourselves this day whom you will serve, whether the gods your ancestors served beyond the Euphrates, or the gods of the Amorites, in whose land you are living. But as for me and my household, we will serve the Lord.
>
> **Joshua 24:15 (NIV)**

I made the decision that day to follow Scripture. I was going to love Jesus, and my household will serve the Lord. I knew that if I focused on that, God would take care of the rest. Even when I moved to East Texas and my daughter stayed with her mom, I knew God was in control. I focused on church, serving God, and sharing what He did in my life. I wish I could say it was easy to do it, but it wasn't.

I had nights I cried and screamed out to the Lord. I shared how hurt I was, how bad this seemed to me to move, and questioned His plan for my life. Don't worry about being honest with God; He already knows. The vulnerability allowed Him to start healing and allowed me to trust Him more. He touched the deepest wounds of my heart, areas that no one really could understand how messed up they were. There is power when we take our issues, feelings, and hurts to Jesus. He is the one who can heal them, but we can't fake it; it takes being honest and vulnerable with Him.

Fast forward five years, and I can say my ex-wife and I co-parent very well. We can work together to ensure our daughter is loved. My daughter has an awesome relationship with the Lord, a great relationship with her mom, a great relationship with her stepmom, a great relationship with me, and she takes faith steps constantly to love Jesus and follow Him. She is flourishing even though she had to walk through hard times.

On one recent Sunday, we were at church sitting together. Our pastor asked us to bow our heads and close our eyes. He asked us to think of a miracle we had seen. "If you have a miracle in mind, raise your hand." He then told us to open our eyes, and miracles were all around us. People could pinpoint times in life that God has moved on their behalf.

Riding home that day, I asked my daughter what her miracle was. I explained she didn't have to share if she didn't want to, but I was curious. Even as I type this, it brings tears to my eyes. My daughter looked at me as we sat at the red light and said directly to me, "My miracle was you, dad. God changed you, and it is the most incredible thing that has happened in my life. You were mean. You expected me to be perfect. You weren't loving. I was scared of you, terrified. You drank all the time, you didn't talk, and when you did, it was usually screaming at someone. I watched God change you! I watched God change your life, and that is my miracle."

I had big alligator tears in my eyes as I looked at her. I thanked her for sharing and told her how proud I was of her. I expressed that I had a lot of regrets but realized God needed to be in control and not me.

By realizing that I don't always have to push and making a choice to let things go, I became a better father. I became more nurturing, loving, and serving. I am thankful for the miracle God did, and with that choice to not control, He showed me how to forgive, let go of past hurts, keep boundaries and responsibility for my household, and to co-parent. I can honestly admit that I am thankful for each trial and challenge because they create a space for God to change my heart and make me more like Him, which is the ultimate desire of my heart.

Chapter Reflection

Holy Spirit, what are You saying to me?

_____
_____
_____
_____
_____
_____
_____
_____
_____
_____
_____
_____
_____
_____
_____
_____
_____

CHAPTER FOUR:

Next Round– Remarriage

The Lord is my shepherd, I lack nothing. He makes me lie down in green pastures, he leads me beside quiet waters, he refreshes my soul. He guides me along the right paths for his name's sake. Even though I walk through the darkest valley, I will fear no evil, for you are with me; your rod and your staff, they comfort me. You prepare a table before me in the presence of my enemies. You anoint my head with oil; my cup overflows. Surely your goodness and love will follow me all the days of my life, and I will dwell in the house of the Lord forever.

Psalm 23:1–6 (NIV)

I wish I could begin this chapter by stating this verse became my life verse when I found out there wasn't going to be restoration in my first marriage. I wish that I trusted the Lord and that I lacked nothing. That He would make me lie down and rest. That He prepared a table for me, but I really was hurt, and I didn't listen to those around me. I didn't want to talk to the Lord. Being a newly single parent, I didn't think He really had my best interest in mind or was able to comfort me, and, to be really honest, I just wanted to do things my way.

I remember having the thought of being rejected once again in my life and feeling how bad I just wanted to be wanted. I craved being in control and having the power to choose for myself what I was going to do. The enemy is tricky when he plants seeds. I was falling for his tricks, and there was no one who could tell me otherwise.

I remember being extremely angry with the Lord because He didn't fix my marriage, didn't save my daughter from pain, and I faced rejection (a very deep root of pain) once again in my life. I remember telling myself to rely on the Lord, but I was so angry and decided, "What is the point?" Scripture tells us, *"Be alert and of sober mind. Your enemy the devil prowls around like a roaring lion looking for someone to devour"* (1 Peter 5:8, NIV).

As the seed of rejection was planted, my mind started thinking, *How can I fix it?* Instead of relying on the Lord, I had sin start to creep in. I made a predetermined decision that I was going to find a way for someone to want to be with me. I knew I would be using them, but it didn't matter to me at the time. I justified the idea in my head and kept telling myself that it won't hurt anyone; everyone else in the world seemed to do it, and it was fine for them.

I didn't see people in my past walking through the pain I was in, so it is fine. It's funny to me how much we can deceive and lie to ourselves. We find justification, and then we withdraw from those who have the ability to speak into our life. I started to search online for dating websites. My thought was, *If I could find a woman who would want me, not reject me, and I could control it, the pain would be a lot less.* I was so wrong, but at the time, no one could tell me. Pastors, friends, and family all tried to tell me not to go down this path, but I would pretend to hear it and say whatever wrapped the conversation up as quickly as possible.

Don't Look Where You Shouldn't

I was married for just over eleven years and together with my first wife for about eighteen years. I had no clue how to date because I was out of the game for so long. One thing I did know was that having online dating sites would make it better because I wouldn't have to walk through rejection face to face; that seemed smart at the time. I created an account on Bumble because it is one of the websites where women request to date men. I thought, *Okay, I won't be rejected, and I could find someone to hook up with and feel better.*

I had a few requests but decided that the first one that wanted to talk and go out, I was going to sleep with them. I remember being nervous and excited because a part of me felt like I missed out on this. There was excitement thinking about walking in sin and getting what I wanted. I was married to my high school girlfriend, and this was my chance to feel like a college student and go out and date.

I was so depressed that I was trying to recreate my past and what I thought I missed in it. Even today, as I write this, I see how broken this thought process was. I was reaching the pathetic stage in life because of the pain that I was walking through.

I went on a date and, the first night, I stayed over. I did everything to manipulate it, including a nice dinner, a bottle of wine, and just coming up to see their place and watch a movie. I was a salesman that night, and to my surprise, I could play the game with the best of them.

We act like it is okay for a guy to be a player, but after

that evening, I realized I turned into what I resented. I was the player—I used people to get what I wanted without ever considering how it would impact them. I remember talking about my faith, how the divorce was not my fault at all (trust me, I contributed to the divorce), and bragged about the financial status I had in my job. I was discussing my motorcycle, trips I took, boat, and house in a gated community. I really laid on what a catch I was; what a dirtbag move because most of it was surface level. Deep down, I was hurt, trying to cope with the pain, and hiding any real feelings.

That next day the woman told me she had to go out of town for two days and would I watch her dog. I said sure and just left the dog in my fenced backyard for two days with a bowl of food. The dog was old and needed to be actually watched, but I didn't care and lied about the care I did provide.

I was in my bathroom looking in the mirror and thought, *Man, what you are becoming. You have sold yourself short, Doug. You are better than this, but you keep making mistakes.* I still wasn't ready to change, and we went out the night she got back. The embarrassing part is that I had the nanny stay to watch my daughter. I skipped out on time with my daughter so I could make myself feel better. I was becoming a terrible parent and an even worse person. Paul identified himself as the chief, highest-ranking, and worst of all sinners, but I was catching up as quick as I could.

I wanted to admit the choices I was making were not good, but I kept going. I continued to lie to myself and say, "It is going to be okay. No one is going to see what you are doing. You can get through this; just enjoy this time."

The stress was building so bad, and my gut was not cooperating either. I started to take meds for heartburn and then Imodium to make sure I didn't have to sprint to the bathroom as my stomach was in knots. I was mixing this combination for a few weeks, and I just couldn't get my body under control. But I kept going out, having drinks and high-calorie meals.

On the next date, we were scheduled to go to a concert. I thought, *Let's grab some dinner beforehand.* I picked her up, and we got to the restaurant and sat at the bar. We started talking about work and how the week was. Then I was asked the question, "Tell me about your marriage and divorce." I realized I never filled in any of the details, and at this point, I was tired of the lie, so I just said, "I will finalize my divorce hopefully soon." She looked at me puzzled and yelled in the bar, "*Wow!*" I was so confused. "What was the problem? I told you I wasn't with her." I told her that we didn't live together, but what I forgot to ever mention was that technically I was still married.

She went on to say, "What the heck am I? I am a mistress! I am sleeping with a married man, and you didn't even tell me. When you talked to me, you said you were recently divorced." (I did say that to avoid the grey area of separation.)

I really didn't know what to say and was acting like, "what is your problem all of a sudden." I became really short and rude to her, saying, "You are making this a big deal. There is nothing wrong with how I am acting," which was completely wrong! We went to the concert in Fort Worth. It was packed, and I was thinking, *Okay, what is the rest of the night going to look like?* On the ride over, we didn't say a word, and when we got there, we didn't even sit next to each other.

The concert started with the steel guitar, and the place erupted. We had reserved seats in the front, and the waitress asked if we wanted anything to drink. I ordered a Sprite, which I hate because, to me, it tastes like sweet water. My stomach was jacked, and the stress of being confronted about having a mistress was so hurtful because it was true.

I felt my stomach start to knot up and twist and turn

again. I was thinking to myself, *This could be bad. Please don't let me have an accident on this date.* I ran to the bathroom without saying a word about where I was going. When I got to the entrance, there was a long line waiting for about five stalls. I opened the first door and thought, *Nope.* The second one was just as bad. The third was awful, but I couldn't be picky any longer. As I sat there with my insides rotting, I was like, *Okay, how am I going to make it through this? I am sick as can be, stuck at a concert, facing the thought of having a mistress, and on top of that, I need to drive her home.* It was going to be an hour and a half round trip. I wasn't thinking clearly, or I would have ordered an Uber.

There was no way I was going to make it. The best part was I spent almost an hour of the concert in the bathroom. I came out and had to turn right back for round two for another thirty minutes. It was bad, not stomach-flu bad, more like I-think-I-am-going-to-die bad. I came out and asked if we could leave because I wasn't feeling good. It was the most awkward ride home with just music playing, so we didn't have to talk.

As we got to her place, my stomach just turned again, and I knew I had to go to the bathroom again. I asked if I could please use the restroom and her response was, "No way. That is disgusting; you can go somewhere else." I was shocked, but looking back, I get it. I was disgusting for how I actually treated someone else. My hurt allowed me to settle for sin rather than focusing on God.

As I drove home that night, I had to stop about three times at different hotels to use their lobby bathrooms. I felt like a hobo just coming in trying to find the restroom and not even be a customer. I got back in my car, and that is when the stress really hit me. I was about to throw up, but there was nothing left. I called my dad and told him I didn't feel good. Calling him at two in the morning as a thirty-five-year-old man to say I am sick really didn't make sense. I had no idea what to do, but he said, "Go to the ER. I am sure you are going to be okay, but there isn't much I can do here."

I pulled into the ER close to my house and checked in. It was about 2 a.m. by the time I made it after the bathroom tour I took from driving her home. They came in and took my blood pressure. The nurse then took it a second time. She was shocked and told me to sit in the chair and please don't move. As I sat there, I felt the right side of my body start to shut down. I was having trouble speaking, and I felt so weak. Another nurse came in and said, "Sir, I am the nurse supervisor. Is your blood pressure normally high?"

I replied, "Never. I have never had blood pressure issues." She just told me my blood pressure was around 235 over 135; it was close to that, if not over. I was out of it by this moment, and it was hard for me to understand what was happening. The level was really high, and my face was starting to droop. I was then taken back where they were concerned; I was going to have a stroke with how high it was.

I was lying on the uncomfortable cotton sheet, of the hospital bed, with a 200-thread count, thinking, *Is this how it ends?* I could feel my body shut down, and I realized that I was really going to die. The Lord reminded me that, during the divorce, I asked Him to take His hand off me, and He did. He told me right then, "This is your life without My presence. I took My hand off you, and you are finally seeing how bad it is when I don't cover you. You are going to die here in this hospital bed, you will not see your daughter again, and you sinned and rejected Me. This is what it is to be a prodigal."

I started to cry and begged God to give me one last shot. I asked Him that if He saved me, I would dedicate the rest of my life to His will no matter what He asked me to do. I told Him that I repent from my sins, for rejecting Him, for pushing my way, and I just want His presence and healing.

Next Round–Remarriage

This was when God met me in my darkest valley. He was my Shepherd, and He was making me lay still so that I could see what happened. As I lay there praying, the Lord spoke clearly to me internally and told me that He would spare my life as long as I did what I promised. He had a plan for my life, and I have been running from it the entire time. He told me I was going to be a pastor, to lead others to repentance, and to share my story no matter how embarrassed or scary it was. He told me that I needed to get rid of sexual sin, get rid of my pride, and focus on His will for my life.

In about thirty minutes, the nurse came in and saw me sitting there with normal blood pressure. They were puzzled and asked if I still had any numbness or loss of feeling. I told them no. I went home about an hour later, messaged the girl I was sleeping with, and ended it. I then slept for about four days straight, and when I got up, I asked my pastor and friend if I could visit him in East Texas. He told me it would be great to visit, he was praying for me, and he knew what I was walking through because he had been in a very similar situation previously.

That week I packed a bag and drove to Longview. As I was driving, I got another dating request and thought, *Okay, this time coffee, public place only, and let's make sure we keep accountability with my pastor and group leaders.* I was going to set physical boundaries that couldn't be crossed and tell my spiritual authority about it. I checked into the hotel and finished some grad schoolwork before meeting my pastor to do some projects at his church and the school they owned. As I pulled into the parking lot of the school, I stopped to pray and ask God, "What is next?"

God told me to be honest with him. To share with my pastor everything that happened and that I needed to repent. "You need to apologize for the lying, for ignoring wisdom, and ask him for help." I met my pastor, and he put me with the youth pastor to fix windows. As we worked, I spilled everything to him. The mistakes of my life, the choices I made, and the reason why I was in Longview. We are still friends to this day; however, I thought the guy would never want to talk to me again because I just was an open book.

My pastor came back after a few hours and walked with me. He asked if I had repentance or remorse. I told him I was repenting. I told him I had another date scheduled, but I wanted to do it the right way. I also told him I probably needed to cancel that date because it didn't feel right after what I did. I promised him I would cancel the date before it came, just let me get through the weekend

Next Round–Remarriage

and reset away from all my mess in the Fort Worth area.

I remember something so specific about this conversation, though. My pastor asked me what I wanted in life, and my response was, "I don't need someone in my life to feel approved of. I am swearing off women because I know I need to do things right. If God wants me to be married again, He's going to have to put her on a platform at church. He will put her on the stage at church leading." We wrapped up the conversation, and he invited me to worship practice that night since a night of worship was coming up. I told him it sounded good and asked if I could drive him so I didn't have to be alone.

As we walked into the church that night, I could hear the worship team practicing. I was looking around the church, thinking it was small but looked really good since they were adding a new coffee shop and kitchen. As I walked into the worship center, I saw a woman on the platform singing and leading. I clearly heard in my head God say, "That is your wife!" The Holy Spirit hit me so hard that I remember saying out loud, "Who is that?" and my pastor hit my chest and said, "Don't worry about it." I really didn't even take a good look at her and was thinking, *What is happening?*

As they finished up, this woman stepped down and

started talking to my pastor. I looked at Pastor Tim and just sat waiting when he then asked her, "Where are your kids this weekend?" She said they were with their dad, and she was focusing on the night of worship and staying with her parents while they were gone. I remember thinking out loud and said, "Wait, you are divorced?" She told me she was, and I couldn't believe it because she looked really young to be divorced and have kids. My pastor then introduced me to Laura and said, "This is my friend Doug."

That night we all went to dinner at On the Border, and I ran to the bathroom. Without me knowing and later hearing from my wife, Pastor Tim wasn't going to sit the two single people together because he didn't want us to feel pressure. Laura looked right at him and said, "I can handle this." We had a great time and discussed divorce, kids, and the movie *Beauty and the Beast*. It just came out, and I asked Laura to go see it the next night. She agreed, and then I asked the table because I was panicking about a date and thought I would see if anyone else wanted to join. They all politely passed. As we left that night, Pastor Tim said to me, "Guess you have a date tomorrow night? Don't mess it up, man. She is so important to my church and me. I need you to understand I am trusting you with the future of my church." What I didn't know was that Laura's family worked at the church, parents were heavily involved, and he was going to have to vouch for me.

The next day I asked Laura to eat dinner before the event. She said she had an early call time but let's go to lunch. As I sat there and we shared our story, I realized how beautiful she was. She loved the Lord, had an amazing journey, and was so nice to me. Pastor Tim texted her beforehand and told her to be a good friend. He explained that I was really hurt and that I really needed a good woman who could be my friend. He expressed that I wouldn't be on the market long because I was a really good guy who just has been really hurt.

That night we went to the movie. On the way home, I decided, *Okay, God, here we go.* I explained to Laura that I wanted to date her. My goal is to have a wife that loves the Lord and will serve in ministry. I told her that I had never built it on a firm foundation and that I always slept with whoever I dated beforehand, but that was not going to happen here. "I will not sleep with you before marriage." I look over, and Laura is crying. I thought, *God, that isn't what was supposed to happen. She was going to be happy*, I thought. Laura expressed to me that she had been waiting for someone to say that to her. She wanted to build this on the proper foundation with God in the middle. We both had dates already scheduled with other people that we both agreed to cancel. I had the finalization of my divorce three weeks out from then. We agreed to be friends, to cross no physical boundaries, and when my divorce was finalized, we would pray and fast about being married. When my divorce was finalized, we had a word from the Lord after praying and fasting. God told me, "This is the woman I have for you. If you do this right, she will serve in leadership at church with you, support your call to pastor, and be your biggest fan as you chase after Jesus." He was so right. We got married five months later and have just celebrated five years together. It has been an amazing journey, and there is so much healing and blessing I would need another book to explain. I am grateful God took me from a place of sin to a place of repentance to a place of blessing and favor. The same can happen for you if you decide to lay the right foundation and build on His Word over your will.

When to Introduce Kids

One thing I was worried about was the timing of introducing my daughter to anyone I dated. I really wasn't sure how to approach it, but God helped me. As Laura and I started to talk and build our friendship, my eight-year-old daughter would constantly ask, "Who are you talking to and texting with?" I explained to her that I had a new

Next Round–Remarriage

friend. I expressed that, with the divorce happening, I was going to date, but if I met someone, it would be a friend, and if we got close, then I would introduce her. I expressed to my daughter that no one can replace her mom and dad as her parents, but God can give us extra people in our lives that care about us. I explained that love is not limited, and even though our family would look different, I asked her to love whoever stepped into our life. I told her that if her mom or I got remarried, people could love her and be a bonus parent, not a replacement. I think it is important to get the thought of competition out of your kid's head as soon as possible. We don't compete with each other for God's love; He loves us all. I didn't want my daughter to feel there was limited space in her heart or that a new stepmom would replace her biological mom.

As things progressed and we were talking more, my daughter started asking questions about Laura. She wanted to know her name and how we met. She wanted to know if we had things in common and if she had kids. My daughter prayed for siblings for years, even before the divorce. I asked Laura if I could share some information, and that is when she won me over.

She sent a text to me for my daughter, saying, "Hey, sweet girl. Your daddy and I are becoming very good friends. But we want to get to know each other as friends first, because that is the best way to start a relationship, by being a good friend. Because we are starting to behave as friends do, we talk on the phone, text each other, and share our day. We talk to God together also. We also decide, as friends, that we won't kiss each other. If we decide to date, we may kiss on occasion. But we will respect each other's bodies and not do anything else. We believe that we can honor God by saving our bodies for marriage. The Bible is very clear about how to behave physically before getting married, and we want to obey God and set a good example for our children. Your daddy is very special to me and a very good friend. I am thankful to have him as my friend, and I promise to always be a good friend to him no matter what."

Laura told me I could read that to her and because we set boundaries on not being physical that if God tells us no, we won't date but gained a good friend in the process. This was mind-blowing to me. I never thought having boundaries would save pain later down the road in dating, but it was working. I wouldn't have to worry about hurting my daughter if I respected the boundaries because there would never be any awkwardness since we wouldn't have dated without praying and fasting and getting a word to marry each other.

I would highly recommend everyone who is single or single again to take this approach. Your kids have already been through enough, and maybe your ex-spouse is dating and introducing people to them. The problem is your kids have faced a broken home, and the only way to keep hurting them is by introducing people in and out of their life.

So, once we got through the process of a few weeks getting to know each other, we decided to pray and fast. It was a long few days, but I really wanted to seek the Lord. I didn't want to be divorced again. The Bible says,

> Two are better than one, because they have a good return for their labor: If either of them falls down, one can help the other up. But pity anyone who falls and has no one to help them up. Also, if two lie down together, they will keep warm. But how can one keep warm alone? Though one may be overpowered, two can defend themselves. A cord of three strands is not quickly broken.
>
> **Ecclesiastes 4:9–12 (NIV)**

I have done it the wrong way in my first marriage. Not only did we not respect physical boundaries, but we didn't build it with God in the middle. By praying and fasting before introducing my daughter to Laura, I had a word now and knew the pain would be missing because we were doing it in God's way. I also knew once the Lord told me to marry Laura that if God stays in the middle and we build the foundation on it, we wouldn't face the divorce rate of 72 percent for typical second marriages. It would take us focusing on God to make it work. We finished praying and fasting, and both had a word from the Lord. God was very clear that we were going to lay a solid foundation, get married, and take big faith steps toward God. Once we had a word, then we knew we could talk to the kids about our plans and build a relationship. It was the best way to do it because then I could share God gave me a word to date Laura, it is someone you will get to know, and my goal is to marry her. It took opinion out and put God's word first.

Meeting the kids the first time was definitely strange. They were little people that I didn't know. They had different personalities, but I knew God told me to treat them well. God told me to treat them like they were my kids but not to replace their father. This was hard because they were not warm, which we will discuss in further chapters, but I knew that since I had a word, I would be there for them. It would take time, patience, and consistency, but our family would blend. I knew having another adult who loved them and could model a good relationship with the Lord was what they needed, so my focus became on chasing God and modeling it for the kids. This built a firm foundation for them as well, and over time, they started to trust me. As the years passed, I saw my heart grow for each of them. I love them just as much as my daughter, and it is an honor to be their stepdad/bonus dad. We laugh, we have deep discussions, we have issues at times, and we are now family!

Unpacking Baggage

As I was walking through my divorce, I decided to take steps to get healing so I didn't bring my issues into another marriage. There is one common issue with someone that has been divorced five times; it is you! To prevent that, I knew that I had some baggage from my past I was carrying, and I needed to let the Lord heal me with it. First, I got in a small group at my church with other people who were remarried and had been through similar things. Second, I found an amazing Christian counselor who could walk me through my thoughts and point me back to Scripture when I would get off track. By taking these steps, I was able to discuss my issues with friends and an independent person who had no dog in the hunt. Last of all, I became very vulnerable. This was the hardest part. I didn't hide the mistakes I made, past hurts I never told anyone, or my feelings, whether justified or not. Please hear me, though;

I didn't share this with everyone, just with trusted people who would help me grow and get healing.

The pain associated with the divorce and my own personal failures in life showed me there was a lot that needed to be undone. I could recognize that I made poor decisions, but I also realized there was pain that I took on even though I didn't cause it. It may not be your fault, but it is your fate. Even if the pain is not your fault, what you do with it and how it affects your life is your responsibility.

I clearly remember one night, I was just in a bad mood. I was blaming everyone else for what I was walking through. I was bashing my soon-to-be ex, I was complaining about the hurt of my childhood, and I was spiraling and heading towards more bad choices. I had my group leader ask me to come on by his house and visit for a few minutes. He didn't live far away, and I thought to myself, *Good, he is going to side up with me and tell me how right I am.*

I headed over there on a really warm Texas day. It was a beautiful drive with winding roads, and I was on my motorcycle. As I pulled into his driveway, I parked my bike on a pad of concrete and saw he was in the back by a pond. The pond was about halfway full of a few ducks just sitting on the water. I walked up to him, and he didn't waste any time. He said, "Doug, I have been thinking and praying. There is something I need to say to you. You aren't going to like it, but you need to hear it. It is time to get over all your hurt. It is time you start dealing with it and stop playing a victim. Was it bad? Yes. But the real question is this. Are you going to let it wreck your life and impact your future, or are you going to deal with it, stop being negative, and build the life you want with the help of Jesus Christ?"

I was so mixed in my feelings. A part of me really wanted to yell at him, punch him in the face, and leave and just state that is what people do; they hurt you. Proverbs states, "Wounds from a friend can be trusted, but an enemy multiplies kisses" (Proverbs 27:6, NIV).

I remembered that verse from church that week. It stood out to me because I remember asking God to put people in my life that would help me, not tell me what I wanted to hear. I didn't like it as much at that time, but it wasn't about my feelings. As Chris Hodges says, choices lead, and feelings follow. So, I made a choice that day. I knew he was my friend; I knew he wanted the best for me, and I knew he was sharing the mistake that he made that took years off his life.

I told him he was right, but I didn't know how to fix it. How do you get through the deep hurt and move on? I asked him what helped, and he said, "I just got extremely honest about it and let Jesus heal it." We discussed that I could share my pain or process, but it was not allowed to be negative or blaming. I would own my own parts, and I would let Jesus shine His light on the pain I had to face.

By taking these steps and being honest, I could use my small group to process how I was currently doing and the areas I needed to grow. I also relied on my counselor, who helped with those areas but started unpacking the pain I had that was never dealt with. As a man, it was hard sharing details of what happened as a child. I was molested as a kid, and I never shared it in my life with anyone. At thirty-five years old, I started to open up, and we did a trauma timeline to unpack what I had carried for so long. With professional help, I was able to walk through the situation and others that were affecting my relationships. I had four close friends that passed away that I really didn't cope with as well as the pain of being abused. This caused me to push people away, avoid asking for help, and rely on building walls to survive, which then led to many unhealthy habits in my life.

We worked through intensive counseling, and I attended my first Freedom conference with my soon-to-be wife. While there, the Holy Spirit started to work on me with other pain, such as being called an accident in life because my siblings were so much older. The point of this is not to share all the pain I have walked through but to show you that when you address it, God can heal it. My life is an open book now, and I don't mind sharing my story because my testimony and what I walked through point back to Jesus.

I saw in the healing process that He really was with me when I walked through the shadows, He made me rest, and He was my shepherd. Jesus constantly discusses that we are His sheep, and sheep can bite. We get scared, we wonder, and we can get hurt by our own decisions in life. But we have a healer; we have someone who wants you to be free from the pain so you don't carry it into the next relationship and marriage, and that person is Jesus.

Chapter Reflection

Holy Spirit, what are You saying to me?

CHAPTER FIVE:

Blending Families

Love is patient, love is kind. It does not envy, it does not boast, it is not proud. It does not dishonor others, it is not self-seeking, it is not easily angered, it keeps no record of wrongs. Love does not delight in evil but rejoices with the truth. It always protects, always trusts, always hopes, always perseveres. Love never fails.

1 Corinthians 13:4–8 (NIV)

Blending a family is one of the hardest things I have ever had to do in my life. Let's be honest; kids are not easy. They don't come with an instruction manual, and they change over time as they develop. The hardest piece of this puzzle for me was choosing to parent and unconditionally love children that did not have my DNA or my last name. I also want to give a shout-out to all those who adopt kids as well because you are taking them in and giving them a home after trauma. This is not an easy task, and I believe this chapter will help you as well.

We have been together for over five years, and our family is hitting full speed. It was incredible to see how we molded, but it took time, patience, and consistency to get it where we wanted it to be. It may not be perfect, but it is the best we have ever had. We still have struggles like most divorce people, and progress can still be made. We are working on it even as I write this book.

During this process, the kids would constantly push boundaries, play parents against each other, and even try to compare households, which made it difficult. The good thing I realized early, though, was not to put pressure on myself to make the perfect family. I didn't want to force my way into God's will. I decided to let Him guide me daily and ask the Holy Spirit for help each day.

One of my friends told me a story Andy Stanley shared. He stated that after a long day, he was not prepared to handle being a husband and father. He didn't want to check out when he got home, so each night, when he pulled into the driveway, he would take a few minutes and just pray. We tend to overlook the power of prayer, but it is one of the most beneficial things we can do. While in his driveway, he would admit to God he was too tired to be a good husband and dad. He would ask the Holy Spirit to come in and help him be what his family needed.

Once I heard that, I decided I would do that every day on my drive to pick up kids or head home if I worked longer than my wife. Let me tell you, the Holy Spirit never lets you down. I didn't always like what He had to say, but it gave me the power to go home and love my family and see their needs over my own. I believe if I had applied this early in my life, I would have walked through a lot less pain. I highly recommend you do the same whether you are a dad or mom. Pray for the power of God to help you be the person our kids need. We are seeing a demand for this more and more as kids are questioning everything in their life. The best foundation I could give my kids was modeling my relationship with Jesus.

Give It Time

I remember, one day, our oldest boy was asking me to help him hook up a Nintendo in the bedroom. He was about eight years old, and his mom and I had just gotten married. I was so tired from work but knew it would mean a lot to him. I walked back through the long hallway into the room. The TV was hung on the wall, so I knew that I would want to wrap the cords up and make it look nice. I wasn't in a huge hurry because I had no plans. He came in and watched me and then just started to ask questions. He asked me things like, "Why there wasn't an HDMI on the Nintendo Wii? Why was the TV mounted without having the cords run already through the wall? Why do we have a Wii when his friends have a PS4?" I was careful and thoughtful in my answers. I was giving him the best I had after a long day.

He then paused and said the one thing I really wanted to be offended at. He looked right at me and then said, "If my dad was here, it would have been hooked up in half the time. You really aren't good at this stuff; he is way better." Did it really matter to me? Yes! I was trying to give him my time and attention, but I had to realize what was really going on. Here is an eight-year-old boy who had to walk through his parents' divorce. He wasn't really taking a shot at me, and his dad probably would have done it faster. The point was that he missed having his family be together. Later that week, he shared that it was hard for him to go to a Christian school and that he felt like he was one of the very few that had divorced parents. The struggle was not towards us but that the enemy was telling him his life was different. That he didn't fit in, and his stepdad would replace his dad.

I knew I had to be understanding. I knew that he was facing a lot, and, at that moment, the Holy Spirit showed me again to love the kids who have had their foundation torn from them. Divorce takes away kids' security and safety without us really knowing it. We have to then rebuild it, and the best thing I could do was not remark or say anything towards him. I just finished doing what I was doing, stated that I loved him, and then gave him some space to enjoy his game.

There are tons of these types of stories from each kid. The kids would fight over something, and we had to decide how to handle it. But I knew they were adapting because there was a new authority in the house. They were used to their mom doing everything, and now you are asking them to trust someone they just met. I was struggling with this some and decided what do I do? I called a pastor friend and one of my inner circle guys to come have breakfast. I explained that the situation kept happening. "I am trying to be there for the kids, I am trying to be patient, and I am trying to show them I am all in because God gave me a word to treat them well." He laughed at me in the corner booth at Denny's, where our arms were sticking to the table, and the booth had the fake leather that you start sweating on as soon as you sit down. He said, "Doug, what did you expect?"

I realized at that moment that my internal expectations were for the kids to appreciate all I was doing. That they would see the effort I was putting in and appreciate it immediately. I thought if I gave them all I had, they would receive it. That was not a realistic expectation for kids ranging from two years old to ten years old. I was expecting them to think and act like an adult when they have no clue how to handle our family blending as well. I realized then that I had to just give it time.

Think of the best meal you have ever had. For me, it is Del Frisco's Steakhouse. I love their thick bacon as an appetizer. A marbled ribeye steak cooked medium rare with some cream corn on the side. Let's not forget about dessert; their bread pudding is amazing. I am talking about banana bread pudding with a cup of coffee to finish off the evening. I was trying to have a five-course meal cooked in a microwave. I wanted my family to just blend, trust each other, and love each other because I married their mom. It wasn't the case, and I realized that patience was going to be worked out for me.

As the verse says at the beginning of the chapter, I would have to treat them with love. I would have to be patient, I would have to be kind, and I would have to keep working at it so that it would be what God intended. I couldn't force it to happen quickly; I just needed to give it time.

Give It Space

My wife and I got married in August of 2017. We had one issue, though, when we got married, and that was going to be where are we going to live. Laura was fine with moving from East Texas to Central Texas. On paper, it all made sense. We had a brand-new house on a corner lot in a very nice neighborhood. The neighborhood had an awesome community pool, and we could continue to split time with my daughter 50/50. Laura was in nursing school and could transfer, and I had an amazing government job with full benefits. It seemed like an easy decision. As we prayed, we knew God was calling us to live in East Texas.

We discussed that God was definitely calling us to East Texas, but it would take a year of going week-on-week-off back and forth till the court would change the custody agreement. I was not happy that I had to have two places to live and drive even more; however, this did allow for our kids to adjust. They had a week-on-week-off schedule with me there. I know not everyone will have this, and my point is not that you live a week with your family and a week away, but it showed me how important timing and space are needed to blend families.

That next summer, I moved in, and we were all under one roof. This is where it got interesting. The kids had to adapt to me being there every day. They weren't used to me being there. My daughter came out to visit for the summer, and I was working from home four out of five days a week.

During the school year, it was very easy to work from home because there weren't any kids at the house to distract. Our oldest also could help get kids ready when they got home, and they were pretty independent. During the summer, though, it was a whole new ballgame. The kids wanted to stay inside all day because it was about 102 outside with 90 percent humidity. East Texas summers make your spine sweat. I mean, your shirt is drenched before you even get moving. I didn't blame them, and we had to figure out how to really get some consistency. We discussed kids needed to do chores, eat, and read for an hour a day before they could watch TV or play games. However, kids get bored really quickly, and when there is an age difference of eight years, they like to do and watch different things.

The kids would constantly ask me to correct the other. They would bicker at times which is natural for siblings that are home for ten hours a day with each other. I was getting worn out and could not understand why it was hard for me to deal with all of it. I decided I needed to discuss possibilities with my wife and explain what I was facing. For me, summer and working from home could be easy. My daughter would watch TV, eat what I made her, and then go back to TV while I worked. The nanny would pick her up and take her someplace to entertain her and bring her back when I was done with meetings. But this was new to me. There were so many kids at the house, and it seemed like they constantly were disagreeing. I was starting to get overwhelmed.

Laura came home, and I was almost in tears as I tried to talk to her. I was afraid she would take it the wrong way. I was worried that I was failing as a stepdad. I didn't want to disappoint her, and I didn't want to feel like I passed my capability. As we sat down, Laura just listened to me as I shared my feelings and what was happening.

Laura is a great listener and communicator, and she is patient with me. She didn't get defensive about her kids or mine. She didn't tell me, "Too bad you decided to marry me." She actually did something I never expected. She smiled big and started to laugh. Laura saw the issue for what it was. I grew up with siblings much older than me. My brother was nine years older, and my sister was eleven. I grew up very much like an only child. We had conflicts, but I was still left to my own stuff when I was a kid and became independent. As a parent, I only had one daughter that, for the last eight years, I focused on. She started to laugh and said, "Doug, why do you try to handle every conflict, disagreement, or request? It isn't possible to fix everything, and sometimes they just need to learn how to work through it as siblings."

I was blown away. I never really thought of it that way and never saw the benefits of letting siblings figure out how to navigate relationships with each other. She could see that this was an important life skill she picked up coming from a big family. She saw the benefits of having multiple siblings with different personalities and identities so that she could connect with anyone. She told me to just give it some space and watch what happens. The kids will feel like you aren't overburdening them, and about 75 percent of the issues they face, they will find a way to work through it. I was grateful that my wife could discuss what the kids really needed and that she could use emotional intelligence over logic on how to handle the situations.

As time went on, it got way easier knowing that I didn't have to fix every issue and I could give them some space. I knew the kids would each be different, and I could learn about their personalities as I spent time with them. I also realized that I didn't allow my daughter the independence she needed when she was an only child. In all seriousness, I was still cutting up her food, opening ketchup packets, and hovering as my daughter was growing. By having a large family now, I had to teach her independence by giving some space and allowing mistakes to be made in a safe environment so that she could grow and learn. Laura constantly would encourage me to let her take some risks and to allow her to learn. It was good for her, and her confidence grew because of it.

As time went on, I still struggled internally at times for not being enough. I felt that the space given might be seen as being non-caring or absent. I think I was still taking on a lot of blame at this time for my marriage falling apart and didn't want it to happen again. I was battling control versus growth. Craig Groeschel, in many messages and his leadership podcast, states, "You can have growth, or you can have control; you get to choose." I met with the same pastor friend as before, and this time we chose Cracker Barrel over Denny's; I opened up about how the enemy was attacking me for this. We sat at a table in the corner of the restaurant with all the fake old-time pictures around us, and I shared, "I am trying to give kids space, but it makes me feel like I'm not there all the time." I expressed my concern about the kids feeling that I wasn't an involved parent, but I also didn't want to micromanage them.

He is a very wise friend and told me a few truths that day. He stated that I need to step in if someone is in danger of being injured or if it gets too serious with the disagreement and can ruin their relationships. Next, he explained to me how he handled parenting. I trusted his advice because he had an amazing relationship with all of his sons. I was mentoring one of his sons, and he would always express how close he was to his dad and that he wanted to follow his example. I knew that I could trust this advice, and it would be helpful because he always points me back to Scripture.

He told me, "Doug, the kids don't need you to be in everything they do day to day. Especially in summer when they are home all day. What they need is to know you are there without being there. They need to know that if you are working in your office and they really need you, you will do what they need. They need to see time and time again that you don't force yourself into their issues but allow them to work through them and then discuss later or guide them in a loving way. What the kids need is space with you being available whenever they ask."

He took this approach with his kids, and it worked. God doesn't force His will on us. He allows us room to make mistakes, screw up, and learn. God will allow us to fail because it is part of the maturing us. He will discipline us when needed because it can grow us. God is sovereign, and He uses everything we do. However, in our hardest times, our times of need, He is always right there when we ask.

He explained that God is a loving Father who never pulls His hand away. He is there, and all we have to do is ask for it when we get to that place. I started to give myself some grace then, and I could see that I was a good father. I provided for my kids, loved my kids, and gave them room to learn and make mistakes without dominating them or micromanaging them. My relationship with the Father allowed me to become a better father. It is hard to give them space at times when they are teens, and you know that it isn't the best decision. The best thing I can do is not just be hard on them but point them back to the Father; to address the heart issue rather than the behavior. Giving space allows room for the Holy Spirit to work, and it worked at blending our family. You will have to pray through it, and if God tells you that you are disengaged with your kids/stepkids, then lean into them and be the parent they need. If God is telling you that you are trying to get kids to perform a certain way and micromanaging everything they face, then listen to Him and give space with guidance. Cover your kids with prayer. It gets easier over time.

Be Consistent

During the first two years of marriage and parenting stepkids, I would constantly pray about how to treat them. They lived in my house, and I knew that I had to be the best parent I could be for them. The hard part was our kids were living in two different households. The rules were changed week to week for them because it was different parents and different homes. We were discussing the issues with this and decided to ask out a counselor for some advice. I remember calling him and discussing the issue with consistency. Laura is very flexible, something that I am not.

Let me give you some insight. I will put more on my plate to be consistent than adapt to a plan that makes my life easier because it bothers me to change more than it does to actually have more responsibility. Let that thought sink in.

For example, our church does a yearly men's conference. It is so hard for me to let things go because I enjoy being involved with them more than I need to be. I don't mind having people help me where it is not my strength, but when it comes to giving prizes away, I love being in the process.

I will run all over town and get every little giveaway because it's something that fills my cup. I have plenty of friends and church members who can do this, but I like handling it. Once I have the major prize in my head, I can't get off it. I wanted to give a brand new 4X4 ATV away this year at our conference, but there was none around.

I spent days on the phone trying to find one, and because of COVID, manufacturers stopped making them. We had limited inventory, and I was determined to find a new ATV. It was hard to find what I was looking for, especially since I was on a limited budget on top of where we were located. Worst of all, I didn't want a used one. I found one locally that had two hours on it, and I refused to get it. The thing was mint and had a manufacturer warranty on it, but I was not willing to settle for less than what I determined previously. I set expectations so high that it was really hard to make it happen. All because I wanted to say new four-wheeler.

I ended up passing on it and spent another two weeks of phone calls to find one almost two hours away. I had to schedule a day to pick this thing up, clean it off, and get all the paperwork, and, in the end, it had an hour and a half of run time because of the setup and maintenance building it. I doubled down and lost time, some extra cash, and took one that was not the preferred color because I didn't want to adapt. Maybe I am the only one who is like this, but control is a hard thing I constantly have to battle against. Once I let go of it, though, I usually am more relaxed, see a better result, and can move on. I'm working on it, so don't judge me.

The same things can happen at home, where I try to control, but control doesn't mean you are consistent. I would come out upset because they didn't finish something that was on the list. They rearranged the schedule but were getting everything done; this sent me on a tailspin because I thought I was clear when I explained it. It made sense in my head. I was being consistent on the result but not the process or expectations. As we met with the counselor, I realized I was trying to control the people in my household and that my wife was adapting, trying to meet my expectations. She was getting hours toward her degree and working at the hospital. The kids were struggling because they felt like at one home, it was a certain way, and at another, it would be different. I was struggling because it felt like adapting constantly. The kids were pushing back at times, and I was tired of grounding for long periods of time because we agreed not to spank each other's kids when we got married. We could take privileges away, though, to enforce the rules we had in our house.

This was when the counselor suggested we create a

constitution (see Appendix). The counselor stated he had a family constitution that he wrote with his wife for their kids. He discussed that it explained what their hope was for the kids, explained privileges came with responsibility, and clearly labeled chores. It worked on a daily basis, and it was going to sound too simple to someone not open to it. He expressed that they worked it on a light system of green, yellow, and red. That each day the kids start with a green light. If they do what they are clearly supposed to in the constitution, then there won't be a problem. They will have privileges, and they won't lose them. He expressed that it would take pressure off of us to keep discipline for long amounts of time and show them daily that there are consequences for our choices. I knew it was simple, but it was also brilliant. This took the pressure off of me, made clear expectations for my family, and my wife created a chore chart and explained it to the kids. It was done in a loving way that changed the way we operated as parents.

The next evening after our session, we completed the constitution and discussed it with our kids. We discussed that, as parents, we had a difficult job. We wanted our kids to become who God designed them to be. We expressed that increased responsibility which included doing chores, completing homework, and choosing a good attitude, gave you freedom. The more they grew, the more responsibility they would have. But with that responsibility, they would have the freedom to do what they choose, and this is the best way we can get them into adulthood. Our desire for the kids, like most parents, was to see kids grow up healthy, loving the Lord, and serving people. We focused on those areas as our heart for any hard discussions we had when they were in trouble. When they had a poor attitude, we discussed it and the choices they made. When they didn't do chores, they lost privileges such as TV, phone, or going over to a friend.

This approach of explaining our heart, having it in writing, and being clear did a couple of things for our family. First, it made us consistent in what we taught our kids and how we disciplined them. It allowed us to pull out the constitution and have discussions with them on why we decided what we did. Second, it allowed the kids to start over daily for poor choices. It allowed them to see we would be consistent with grace as much as we were with punishment.

Last of all, it helped the kids see consistency in our household without us having to manage them or control them. This simple system allowed us to speak to their heart and identify that we really did care.

We have used this for the last three years, and it has

been a game-changer for us. I wish I would have had this tool when I was growing up. Each kid has their own personality, and we were able to use this system to be flexible enough to work with each one but consistent in the values we were teaching them.

The kids will argue this system and roll their eyes when you present it. They won't understand that you are trying to parent them differently than others. I was told because I said so when I was growing up, but rules without relationships lead to rebellion. I want my kids to avoid rebellion if they can. I want them to be in a relationship with me. The best relationship we can provide is the same as our Father in heaven, which is consistent. He is always there, and He is always teaching us, showing us grace, disciplining us when necessary, and loving us unconditionally. I hope the example constitution will help you co-parent kids if you are remarried and feel free to adjust based on your kid's needs, your family values, and your desires. There is no perfect plan, but without a plan, you are just rolling the dice on results. I am not willing to gamble with their future; they matter and are going to change the world!

Chapter Reflection

Holy Spirit, what are You saying to me?

CHAPTER SIX:

Fighting for Unity and Peace

"Finally, brothers and sisters, rejoice! Strive for full restoration, encourage one another, be of one mind, live in peace" (2 Corinthians 13:11, NIV).

I want to be very clear before we dive into this chapter, unity doesn't mean you have to agree, have complete restoration, or be in uniformity. To have unity and peace, I would encourage you to find a way to move forward and come to a resolution that works for everyone involved. To have unity, you don't have to give up boundaries or change your position; you just have to listen to the Holy Spirit, find common ground, and move past the conflict once it occurred. You can stand your ground in an argument if the Holy Spirit tells you, but in most cases, our opinion or perspective drives this.

Don't Take the Bait

Conflict can cause a few things that are beneficial as well. It can help you see a different perspective; it can create clarity at the moment, and last of all, it can allow you to find creative solutions. When we view conflict differently, it can allow us to embrace it without seeking it out or creating unnecessary conflict. Unhealthy conflict just causes fighting, yelling, and bulldozing your way past a better future. That is not what I mean by conflict. I am discussing when you don't agree and see eye to eye at the moment, decision, or path forward.

When you get remarried and start to move forward after a divorce, you will face different conflicts with yourself and your beliefs, with your spouse, with your ex-spouse, and last of all, with kids. This is inevitable because everyone thinks differently, has different viewpoints, and all parties involved have to adjust, whether they choose the divorce or not. The key is to navigate through it and allow the relationship to build so that, over time, you can have trust. I know what you are thinking, mostly because I thought it too. How can I ever trust the person that hurt me, left me, or allowed this to happen? The truth is there are faults on both sides in a divorce, and if you feel that way, it most likely falls on you still getting healing and health. I never thought my wife and I would have dinner with my ex-wife to discuss our kids' future. See, my ex-wife hugs my wife and says, "It's good to see you," or have the three of us stand in front of my daughter's school to lay hands on our child and pray for her as she goes into high school; but God has allowed healing, forgiveness, and healthy boundaries to co-parent even when there have been conflicts.

Conflict with Spouses

I can remember the first conflict I had with Laura. Actually, it was when we were dating and had a long talk on the phone. I was pacing around the house, answering some pretty deep questions about my beliefs and faith. We were talking through some key values we had when she asked me the question I was avoiding for some time. She asked me, "Are you tithing your income, and is that a key area in your life you believe in?"

I knew that this was going to cause an issue because I understood the biblical principle of tithing, studied it, and wanted to follow it, but I wasn't. I hesitated for a moment on the phone and actually thought about saying I didn't want to discuss it. She could hear my pause and patiently waited for the answer. I told her, "Technically, I am giving away 10 percent of my gross income; however, only five of that goes to the church."

She responded, "Why do you do that?" This is where she is very smart, patient, and wise. She didn't argue with me, lecture me on what is in Scripture, or say I was wrong. She followed up with a question trying to get to the reason. Here is the reason I didn't tithe.

When I was around twenty-five years old, I found a church in our neighborhood that I really liked. It was a non-denomination church, and the real reason I even showed up was that one evening, the pastor stopped at my door, dropped off a pizza, and said he hoped I had a great night and to come to check them out sometime. I was thinking, great, I now took this pizza, so I have to go this Sunday. Guilt worked on me, and I showed up. That lead to a two-year journey of attending, joining, serving coffee, and then eventually sharing my story in front of the church. I was involved with as much as I could be. As I plugged in, the pastor became one of my closest friends.

During this time, in my first marriage, my wife got really sick, and we almost lost her when my daughter was born. The pastor was there to watch my daughter, start a food train, and help in any way possible. If I am being vulnerable, my faith was in him more than Jesus. I wasn't even really saved yet and didn't have a relationship with Jesus till a few years later. As my first wife recovered, I knew I wanted to serve under him. I started to help with our church's new building campaign and gave what I could to raise funds. I started discussing with everyone in the church what this could do for our small town. I really did believe that we were on the right track.

We built the building, and it was going really well. Then one day, he tells me he is leaving the church. I was shocked. On top of that, he partnered with some people that I was not a fan of. They funded him to become a county judge. I was so hurt he left the project; I was hurt that he was accepting more funds from our community instead of staying as he promised when we built the building, and I was mostly hurt because our friendship was strained. I felt like I was misguided, and the use of the funds he had was directed elsewhere.

This wound made me not want to trust the church. I didn't believe the church could really handle large sums of money, and I felt that pastors were in it to gain resources for their own projects. I even treated other pastors poorly because of the pain and hurt I was carrying. As I discussed this with my soon-to-be wife, I realized I was still hurt. She followed up and asked if I would do something for her. She asked me to pray and see if it was time to trust God and do what was biblical no matter what the outcome was.

I knew right then that I needed to tithe the entire amount to the church and let go of my wounds. While praying, I felt the Lord challenge me beyond tithing and become generous in addition to tithing. It changed my perspective, and I will be honest; I keep trying to outgive God but lose every time.

The point of this is not to get you to give money to the church even though it is biblical. The point is to show you the foundation that was set to deal with conflict in our marriage, especially since we were married before. My wife didn't yell at me, lecture me, or guilt me into it. She brought her feelings to me, asked why I decided what I did, and then asked me to go to the Lord and even other authorities to seek guidance and wisdom. When we take this approach, we navigate through conflict so much easier. We are able to discuss where we stand and then fight for unity. There have been times we faced conflict, and she was right, and other times I was right. The point isn't being right; the point is moving forward focused on what God has planned for your family and you.

Even today, when we don't see eye to eye, we create a safe place to take turns sharing what we feel and believe. We express where we stand and what we think the Lord is saying to us. We then will take time to pray about it, and if we can't find common ground, we submit to healthy spiritual authority. We have a few trusted pastors and friends that guide us in our marriage. This has helped us tremendously, especially with such a high divorce rate for second marriages. I would advise you to each take this approach when dealing with your spouse. Most divorced people, you could even say all divorce people, have hurt from prior conflict. The way we deal with it is by seeing it in a healthy way that fights for unity. That allows the Holy Spirit to lead and guide us so that our feelings don't drive us. Again, choices lead, and feelings follow. You can win, or you can be married; the best option is to trust the Holy Spirit because He brought you together.

Conflict with Ex-Spouses

"Honor your father and your mother, so that you may live long in the land the Lord your God is giving you" (Exodus 20:12, NIV).

When writing this section, I was really hesitant. It was hard because, like most of you who are co-parenting and divorced, there has been a lot of conflict with ex-spouses. It could be self-inflicted or even just miscommunication. It might be a hurt person hurting people; either way, there are ways to deal with conflict that will allow you to navigate ahead and find unity without giving up your boundaries.

Above, we discussed strategies such as using five words or less, but in this section, I want to focus on how to deal with conflict and reflect instead of projecting. When we face conflict with ex-spouses, I would advise you both to pause until it can be done without a heated discussion.

The key realization is that the person you are no longer married to still understands you, knows your triggers, and will use them if they are not careful as well. I also will advise women that it is hard to approach this if the man you were married to isn't ready to apply these steps first. I believe, just like marriage, it is the male's responsibility to lead his family. After the divorce, it is his responsibility to lead in forgiveness, repentance, and work at co-parenting after divorce no matter who is at fault. He still is the leader of his children, and even though you are not married to him, it is important that he sets a foundation that honors his children's mother.

By honoring each other, you will find more common ground and a way forward. Please hear me in this, we are commanded by the Bible that we are to honor our mother and father, but it is your responsibility as a parent to model it for the kids once you are divorced. Stop saying negative things, bad-mouthing, or pointing out the faults of the other parent. If hard questions are asked, like why you are divorced, let the other parent discuss their part in it; you discuss your failings. I have had to do this with my daughter even though she knew more than I wanted her to.

I didn't always get it right, and she knew more because, at first, I didn't truly take this approach. It was after time I saw I was hurting her by making her choose sides rather than dealing with conflict in a healthy way. Finger-pointing never leads to a common ground; it only creates more issues when it comes to co-parenting and working together.

One of the biggest conflicts I faced with my ex-wife was that I moved to Longview. Honestly, I understand why my ex-spouse was so angry about it. I could have argued that we are no longer together so I can make my own decisions; I could have said we wouldn't be in this mess if we hadn't divorced. I could have used any excuse I wanted, but instead, I chose to pause.

As I paused and spent time praying, I faced a difficult question. I felt the Lord ask me, "What do you think she is feeling right now?" At that moment, I started to think about the fear I would have had, such as losing my daughter or her being away and not being able to support her. I thought about what I would feel like missing her games, missing school functions, and being apart. It softened my heart and allowed me to see areas that would be a huge concern if I was on the other end.

God also showed me it would be very challenging because I would have felt that my ex-wife didn't stick to her word again. I signed my decree, and at the time, it was less than a year when I was asking to change it. I was changing the agreement and the situation, and this impacted her as well.

One day when we were discussing it, I told my ex-wife that I was sorry that this caused issues and that one day our daughter might want to move out here. She was not happy to hear that and not ready to hear it. She was upset, and let's just say the conversation was not going in a positive direction for both of us. Again, I paused and thought through why she was upset, and it focused on the agreement changing again. I could hear the Holy Spirit say one thing to me, and I said it over the phone. I told my ex-wife that if she ever gets called by the Lord to do something, I hope she says yes and doesn't hesitate because of our daughter or other people's opinion. I ended the call with that and left it there.

A few months later, my wife, Laura, and I sat and had dinner with her and her boyfriend to discuss what it would look like if my daughter did move out here. Because we found common ground on calling and didn't fight to fight, we were able to work through it. The point is this: when you take time to pause, reflect, and gain perspective, the Holy Spirit will show you blind spots. It will allow you to be empathetic to the person who might have hurt you worse than anyone in the entire world. Divorce is the hardest thing I have ever walked through, but in the end, it is now important to honor my daughter's mom. She is a good mother to her and allowed her to move when she wanted to. She has always honored me with our daughter, and because we both take that approach, we can find unity in what is best for her without giving up our own boundaries.

I hope as you deal with conflict with ex-spouses, you will constantly ask the Holy Spirit these few things. Ask Him for wisdom, guidance, a gatekeeper at your mouth, and, last of all, a path forward. God can do much with very little, but we have to be obedient when we ask. It's my prayer that you would learn from my mistakes, and early on in your separation, divorce, marriage, or remarriage, you would invite the Holy Spirit into your conflicts.

Conflict with Kids

When my wife and I married in 2017, it was great. We were happy, found what we believed God had planned for us, and looked forward to blending a family. We had a lot of time to discuss what our goals were, what our family would look like, and how to get there. One evening, though, I was upset and felt the kids were being awful to each other. They were bickering, fighting, and just using the wrong tone when they tried to talk to each other. I was in my room trying to work, and I could hear them in the bedroom next to me going at it. It was about two minutes of straight arguing with each other. I could have walked in there, separated them, and given it time to talk it out, but I was done. As I got out of the chair and headed toward my door, I could feel myself getting angry. I told them a few times to stop, and they weren't listening. Maybe I am the only parent that ever got upset at kids for not listening, but based on my conversations with other parents, we have all been there. Unfortunately, though, I didn't pause before I threw the door open. If I had been intentional with my pause, I could have slowed down instead of blowing up.

I yelled really loud at my stepdaughter and made her just start balling. I can't even remember what I said or how I said it, but I was not in a good place. As she sat back on her bed and began to cry, I walked into my room thinking, *Well, that stopped them arguing.* It was at that moment my wife walked back and asked me if I thought I had handled it correctly. I didn't! I even tried to justify that I am the parent and I am sick of all the kids arguing.

She looked at me and said, "I think it was harsh. I think you need to pray and ask if you handled it correctly or if you just tore a little girl apart when she has had a hard day." I hated that my wife was right, but like most of us, men have realized there are times our wife is right because they are more loving, nurturing, and empathetic than we are as men. The Holy Spirit was yelling at me, too, that she was right.

I got up, walked back out the door, and sat on the bed with my stepdaughter. I told her I was sorry for yelling and getting so upset and that it wasn't the right way for me to handle it. I asked her to forgive me. This was hard as a parent because I never learned how to say sorry to a child. I was raised strict, and I didn't question when a parent yelled. When I asked her to forgive me, she looked up at me and said, "Yes, I do." We talked and agreed it was a long day and everything was just off. As we finished the conversation, her tears turned into a smile, and she gave me a hug. It was one of those moments as a parent that I thought, *Man, I messed up bad, but with humility and correction, it ended better than it started.*

When I got back to our room, my wife was sitting in a chair and said, "Can we talk?" I was worried we would fight about it because I screwed up, and it was already hard enough for me to admit I was wrong. That isn't what happened at all. She asked me questions like, "Why does the conflict bother you?" "What was it like when you were growing up?" and "What really pushed you to the edge?"

I grew up in a different environment than what I was raising kids in. I had almost ten years apart from my older siblings and never really had to deal with them arguing over a toy I had, what to watch on TV, or what we were going to do. My sister was even older than that, and when we would go places, they thought she was my mom. I grew up more like an only child with older siblings who helped you run places and, once in a while, do something fun. We didn't have to face a lot of conflicts since they moved out when I was really little.

When I had my daughter, she was the only one. My ex-wife and I had health complications and decided not to have more kids. I was used to a home with a single child, no conflict, and being the adult and authority that could create the environment. I never grew up in a big family, with older siblings trying to dominate and letting kids just figure out how to navigate their relationships.

As my wife sat there, she listened. She was encouraging and gave me different viewpoints that were created from the conflict. She asked my point of view on conflict and why it was bothering me that our kids weren't perfect and getting along. It was a lot of transition for me to go from one to five kids, and that was all coming up. As we talked, I realized we could navigate better. I don't have to be involved all the time, and I could allow the kids to figure out how to deal with each other. I could remind them not to argue, but they also needed to learn because it is creating life lessons down the road so they can work with others.

I am thankful for the conflict now that I look back. It really did bond the kids and allow them to figure it out. It taught my daughter how to have siblings, be less selfish, and work together when there was conflict. The other night we sat down while the kids were eating dinner. We had already eaten before a school function, but they were hungry again, so they all grabbed tacos from a local restaurant to take home. As we sat at the dinner table and watched them eat, the older ones paused and looked at my wife and me. They both said at the same time, "What is going on? What are we having a family meeting on?" I had to tell them we were not having a family meeting. We were just sitting together and enjoying time with them even though we weren't hungry. It made me smile because, in a short amount of time, our kids realize that we are family. Family will have conflict, they will disagree, but in the end, you move forward with unity and peace. I am so grateful for these kids and grateful for the hard times because, through them, they created a family! One we all desperately needed.

Chapter Reflection

Holy Spirit, what are You saying to me?

CHAPTER SEVEN:

Respecting Boundaries and Trusting Authority

When Jesus had entered Capernaum, a centurion came to him, asking for help. "Lord," he said, "my servant lies at home paralyzed, suffering terribly." Jesus said to him, "Shall I come and heal him?" The centurion replied, "Lord, I do not deserve to have you come under my roof. But just say the word, and my servant will be healed. For I myself am a man under authority, with soldiers under me. I tell this one, 'Go,' and he goes; and that one, 'Come,' and he comes. I say to my servant, 'Do this,' and he does it." When Jesus heard this, he was amazed and said to those following him, "Truly I tell you, I have not found anyone in Israel with such great faith. I say to you that many will come from the east and the west, and will take their places at the feast with Abraham, Isaac and Jacob in the kingdom of heaven. But the subjects of the kingdom will be thrown outside, into the darkness, where there will be weeping and gnashing of teeth." Then Jesus said to the centurion, "Go! Let it be done just as you believed it would." And his servant was healed at that moment.

Matthew 8:5–13 (NIV)

I haven't ever heard someone say that they love boundaries and authority in my entire life. Let's just say it. As an American, I tend to have an authority issue, especially when I don't like it, limits me, or tells me what I have to do. This would not be a popular verse in our society, but it is becoming one of my favorite Bible stories.

I worked for the Army for many years, and during that chain of command was drilled into us. We worked on operation orders, reported to command, and did what we were ordered to do. The chain of command was attractive because it created order and structure, something I enjoy. I am not great at adapting.

I actually can create more work by sticking to the original plan than adapting and being flexible. For example, one night, we had plans to go to dinner with a group of people, drive separate cars, get childcare, and then pay for all of it to celebrate my wife's birthday. I planned it based on what I was told a few weeks prior by my wife what she wanted.

About two days before, my wife said, "Hey, we changed plans, and now just the girls are going, and you can stay home." This made it way easier for me because I was able to stay home and do what I wanted to do. We had dinner planned for later that night, and we celebrated her birthday. The thing that got me was I was upset at first because that was not the original plan. I hate adapting, and it caused me to want to stick to the more difficult plan than just adjusting. Maybe I am the only one like this, but adapting is not my strength.

In this story, you see the situation change when Jesus adapted based on the centurion's response. There are only a few times Jesus recognizes people for having great faith, and this is one of them. I would love at the end of my life for Jesus to tell me I lived my life with great faith. There are a few great points we can draw from the centurion and Jesus as they interacted. Let's cover the points of the story and then apply them to your situation.

The first is that the centurion understood the chain of command and how to respect authority. He discusses that he is used to authority, has experience with it, and he understands the power of his words to soldiers that are under him.

Second, the centurion recognized his source and who could guide him when he was in a challenging situation. He knew God was in control and that Jesus was able to heal his soldier with just a word.

Third, the centurion was quick to listen and had a heart that would allow him to reap what he had sowed. Because the centurion lived a life under authority, he was able to benefit from it when he spoke with Jesus.

Last, the centurion was recognized as having big faith because he didn't require God to do it his way. In my opinion, I am sure the centurion wanted Jesus to come to heal his soldier and visit his house, but he knew that wasn't needed. He had the faith to trust God even when it looked different than expected.

Stick to the Decree

When we apply these principles to our lives, we benefit. We are under the authority of the law, and when we honor it, we are able to avoid unhealthy conflict and arguing. No one likes their decree after a divorce. It doesn't benefit either party, makes you give up areas to have common ground, and can be upheld in a court. But like the centurion, when we respect authority, we allow God to do

Respecting Boundaries and Trusting Authority

His best part. The decree can be long and confusing as well, so I advise anyone who is going through a divorce and reading this to take time to understand exactly what you are signing.

Most disagreements that I have pastored people through after a divorce is because the person isn't respecting the authority that is in place. They don't follow the decree, try to make adjustments that benefit them, and then get upset when they feel the other person isn't staying with it. Please hear me in this; it is not your job to make your ex-spouse follow the decree. It is your job to follow it and stand on it. It may even take attorneys to step in, but when you honor it and honor the authority that wrote it, God starts to work. The boundary we set from the beginning is to trust the decree and work within that. By sticking to the agreed arrangement, we are able to start building trust. This allows for conversations down the road when changes are needed or for some areas to adjust. Over time the decree will become a guideline, but you will not get that in the first year of being divorced. You have to remember that it is not a marriage and family anymore, but more of a business arrangement and contract. That sounds very cold; however, when you approach it that way, you take feelings out that cause heated discussions, arguments, and unhealthy conflict. It allows you time to work together and show each party involved that you will follow what was agreed to. After some time, if you decide to use it as a guide rather than a contract, test it in small areas. If, for some reason, it creates issues, then go back to the decree since it was established to help you in these areas where conflict can occur. The best advice still, though, is to stick to the decree and use your attorneys to make big changes. Also, don't fall on your sword or make a mountain out of a molehill for little issues. Navigate through them and use the decree if common ground can't be found.

For example, in our case, it is easy to get upset about our decrees in summertime. We can discuss it, but a lot of times, the kids being from two separate families will have gaps in the summer where they are split because they are with their other parents. It is not something my wife and I enjoy; it takes a lot of planning to see when we can do stuff with all of them, and it can get complicated. The decree specifically lays out the days the kids have with their other parents, and it really doesn't matter what our feelings are. Just like the centurion, we have to trust that God has it covered, and we need to follow the authority that established it. Having kids gone over different holidays complicates family gatherings and dynamics as well, but it is the best thing; we have to ensure both sides are able to have time with our children.

Respecting Boundaries and Trusting Authority

When you stick to the decree, you avoid grey areas. It is spelled out in black and white and if there is a gap in clarification, ask your attorney. It is better to pay a small fee to get advice than to step out of authority and be uncovered. If we believe in Jesus and the power of His name, then we must agree that God knew what the decree would say. He allowed it to happen even if you don't think it is fair. When you submit to that, it allows God to start working. Don't get in the way of the Holy Spirit; find peace in what was established even when it isn't fully what you wanted.

When it comes time to modify the decree, make sure that you honor the other parent as well. God cares about your heart. When you approach changes, make sure you are prayed up beforehand and pick an attorney who has the same beliefs in getting what is best for the kids no matter what. You can be easily influenced when walking through big decisions like this, so try to find an attorney who has values similar to you, that walks with the Lord, and that knows God never intended this but let's find common ground that the kids will be healthy in the long run.

Watch What You Say

> Do not let any unwholesome talk come out of your mouths, but only what is helpful for building others up according to their needs, that it may benefit those who listen. ...Get rid of all bitterness, rage and anger, brawling and slander, along with every form of malice. Be kind and compassionate to one another, forgiving each other, just as in Christ God forgave you.
>
> **Ephesians 4:29, 31–32 (NIV)**

Please take a moment and read the scripture once again, or if you are like me and skipped over it, please go back for a moment.

Once you walk through a divorce, it can be really hard not to have bitterness, rage, anger, and slander. You will see, as you divide assets and debts, the little things can stir you up. Having scriptures memorized can help you in these situations to choose better approaches at times.

The hardest part of walking through divorce and co-parenting is choosing not to speak negatively, no matter what happens. There will be times you will have to be honest with kids' questions but give your perspective and not try to assume what the other person was thinking or their agenda. It takes practice! Time and time again, I see this become a common ground for parents pushing kids away rather than bringing them close. It may start with pulling the kid in, but down the road, they hear both sides, and both usually are different, which pushes them away from trusting you. No matter what, your kids are still going to want a relationship with the other parent, and you, talking negatively about them, will push them away rather than pull them closer.

I remember a specific time when my daughter came home from her mom's, and she was upset. I could tell that she and her mom had a disagreement, and she was not happy with what was being said to her. It was a hard time for all of us as we were adjusting, but really my daughter was struggling because she could feel the pull from both parents. She felt trapped in the middle no matter what. This was causing an internal conflict for her.

I asked Aubrey what happened, and she explained to me that her mom opened up about why we got divorced. She was vulnerable with Aubrey, and I could tell it bugged her. She owned her mistakes; trust me, we both made mistakes in our marriage, and her mom took the time to discuss it with her and apologize. Her mom was very honoring of me and took the approach of only focusing on her actions and what caused them. I asked Aubrey why it bothered her so much and if we could talk about it. She said it bugged her because why did it have to go so bad? Why did her mom make the mistakes that happened?

I had an option there; I could gang up and win her over, or I could honor her mom and discuss the situation from both sides. I told my daughter that the mistakes made were two-fold. It is never one person's fault when a marriage fails. Each party has a part in it. The seeds we plant grow, and I did not do a great job laying a foundation, loving her mom when we were married, or even choosing to be in a relationship because, for years, I treated it more like roommates.

I expressed to my daughter that her mom was brave to be open and vulnerable and that I have done the same, and she was okay with me. Aubrey thought of it and realized that there was not one side that was right and one that was wrong. I expressed to her that she had been feeling pulled by both sides and apologized for any part I had in that. I explained that she was so young and had to take on a lot of maturity based on having split households. Last of all, I finished by expressing that love is a choice and not a limited resource; that she can love and forgive her mom just like she loved and forgave me when I asked. We talked about how she loved her stepmom, her new siblings, and the extended family she has now. The point is that I tried to show my daughter that there is always room for forgiveness, grace, and love.

I asked my daughter to do me a favor. To really forgive her mom and me and then just work on the relationship she has with both of us. I asked her to love both of us and not put limitations on it. Last of all, I expressed there are biblical reasons for divorce, that restoration did not happen, but God was still sovereign and knew this would happen. He was going to use this situation no matter what.

There was another time I had to watch what I said to my stepson. We were in the first year of blending our family, and I thought the kids would enjoy having a Nintendo Wii hooked up to play some games together. I was excited to hook it up and thought, *This is a great way to connect with him.* Please understand this, he was the oldest boy and was very protective of his mom. He didn't like me; actually, he was constantly looking for things that I did differently or wrong. This wasn't his fault because he was facing a lot of transition and processing through having another male authority in his life who wasn't his dad.

I asked him to join me in the room and help me hook up the Wii. I thought we could talk and spend some time together, so I purposely asked him to help me with each cord. As he handed me the cords, he kept asking me, "Do you even know what you are doing?" I have hooked up game systems since I was a kid; yes, I knew what I was doing. He totally missed the point that I was trying to get him involved in the process and connect.

As we were finishing up, he stopped and looked at me and said, "That took you forever! My dad would have had it hooked up in like two minutes. I don't think you really knew what you were doing."

In my mind, I thought a few things. I was thinking, *I bet your dad can't, especially if you are helping him!* I also thought, *Well, he isn't here!* I could have been sarcastic or ignored it, but instead, I said something to him that even caught him off guard.

I said, "Man, I bet your dad could do it really quick. He probably has way more experience in this than I do. I am glad you were here to help, and I bet you miss your dad a lot." At that time, I was struggling with trying to set my authority, but I could feel the Holy Spirit say be gentle and build him up.

He looked at me and then discussed how it has been hard for him to have two households. He stated that, at school, he sometimes felt like he was the only one with divorced parents because no one ever talked about it. At that moment, I saw him open up, be honest, and share how much change this has caused him.

I wish I could say every aspect of these conversations was positive, but they weren't. The goal, though, for kids, especially as a stepparent, is to not talk negatively about their parents. Your goal is to express that each person can love them, support them, and encourage them differently.

Believe it or not, this applies to ex-spouses too when you are talking with your spouse. How you discuss your ex shows your heart to your spouse. There are times and places to talk to your spouse about the hurt you have been through, challenges that you faced, and mistakes that were made, but that is done sitting together and walking through the process, not during disagreements.

I remember something I had to apologize to my wife about recently. It was over five years old, but the Holy Spirit showed me a time I did not react well to a situation during my divorce and took it out on her. As we were getting divorced, my ex-wife and her family were on my phone plan. They had to separate their lines, and without her ever really knowing, I got a bill for a thousand dollars. Looking back, my ex was always fair with the cost of stuff to divide, but I didn't consider that.

I remember being in the house; at that time, Laura and I were still dating, and I went off. I said how mad I was that she caused this, and I am still paying for it. I was angry and cussed her out in front of Laura about how I had been wronged the whole time. Please hear me in this; it is not a moment I am proud of, and I went full victim here.

I could not calm down, and I got on the phone with AT&T customer service to dispute the charge. They told me that she was authorized as a user to separate her bill. They stated she had fees as well for the new account. They finished by stating that if I didn't agree with the approach, the only way to get around it was to ask for an investigation by looking into fraud charges. That is when it hit me that my offense was getting to a level that was out of control. I wasn't going to press charges; I just didn't want to pay it. In addition, looking back now, I don't believe there was ever fraud, just my anger, bitterness, and resentment.

Laura was sweet and said that it was okay. She stated we could pay it and that this was part of the divorce agreement. She reminded me that my ex-wife paid my legal bills and was fair in the divorce. I calmed down and let it go. It was while I was getting ready for this book that the Lord brought this back. He told me that I needed to apologize to Laura for the way I acted. He reminded me that I was so hurt I only saw one side and that I didn't give anyone a chance to explain.

It was hard to go to Laura and say this. I asked her, "Can we walk the neighborhood? I have something I need to discuss with you." I told her that I was sorry for how I acted and that it wasn't right. My ex didn't deserve it, and she didn't deserve to be on the receiving end of it. I told her how my pride got in my way, and I needed to repent and apologize for this, even though it was over five years ago.

Laura said to me that she remembered that day. She said it showed her how hurt I really was and all the pain I didn't hand over to the Lord. She reminded me of God's goodness that little things like that didn't ruin the course were on to co-parent. She accepted my apology and said she never thought of it again, but I knew it was wrong. I knew I needed to change if God was pointing it out. By admitting my shortfalls and acknowledging the hurt and bitterness I had that day, I was able to heal and forgive myself for taking on an offense that was incidental.

I would encourage you to watch your words. Watch what you say to your ex-spouse, your spouse, and your kids. Words either build up or tear down, but they are not neutral. They create momentum one way or another. Take some time as you finish this section and ask yourself a reflective question. Are my stories, words, and actions building up others as needed, or are they tearing down people and justifying my offense? If they are tearing down, then repent. Pray for forgiveness and ask the Lord to change your path. It is never too late, even after five years, to admit your heart and attitude were wrong and ask for forgiveness. There is grace right around the corner, but it takes humbling ourselves to receive it.

Find Common Ground for Raising Families

> You family of snakes! How can you say good things when you are sinful? The mouth speaks what the heart is full of. A good man will speak good things because of the good in him. A bad man will speak bad things because of the sin in him. I say to you, on the day men stand before God, they will have to give an answer for every word they have spoken that was not important. For it is by your words that you will be not guilty and it is by your words that you will be guilty.
>
> **Matthew 12:34–37 (NLV)**

When it comes to speaking life and raising kids, there are many obstacles you face, especially with respecting boundaries. You will not like the decree when there are gaps that don't fit your schedule, you may not like how your ex-spouse parents or runs their household, and you will find many opportunities to disagree. But as Jesus was saying in Matthew, what your heart is holding will come out of your mouth.

When I walk people through post-divorce discussions and co-parenting discussions, I usually don't address the symptoms. I start with the heart. If your heart is good, then you will hear things in the conversation that points to it. They will state things like, "They are a good parent," "They are trying," "I know they can see it from a different perspective," etc.

When the person doesn't have the right heart, you hear things like, "They always do this; it never changes," "They do this on purpose," "They are full of rage," etc. Even the tone they use in a conversation matters. You can hear it when they speak. The Bible tells us that our fight is not against flesh and blood but against spirits and principalities. If you are finding yourself dealing with evil and not just disagreement, then get police and attorneys involved and stay out of it. If you are just dealing with disagreements, then watch how you speak because it reflects your heart.

The best way to do this is to find common ground for the kids. Things like agreeing that family functions are important and we will work around those to ensure our kids get to see their family as much as possible is a common area to start. Letting parents have an extra day when you don't have plans doesn't hurt anyone and can help build a better co-parenting relationship. There are many areas where common ground can be found, but there are ones you think would be common but don't align with both parents.

Growing up, sports were important to my ex-wife and me. We believe sports can build up kids very well, but as a divorced dad, I believe family time is more important. I can also state the most important thing in our family is our kids are serving the Lord and walking in His ways. That can even cause disagreement in families because there are different ideas in theology, dating, and discipline.

The best way to find common ground is by praying. Pray for your ex-spouse; yes, I know that is difficult, but over time, it becomes easier. Pray for wisdom and discernment on how to find common ground. All these approaches are biblical, and when we lean into the Holy Spirit, He will

Respecting Boundaries and Trusting Authority

show you a way much better than your own.

It will not always be comfortable or the way you want to approach things, but that is okay. The results may not even turn into what you expect, but if you are listening to the Lord and seeking guidance from a spiritual authority, then you can trust God's way is better no matter what. Scripture states, *"But Samuel replied: 'Does the Lord delight in burnt offerings and sacrifices as much as in obeying the Lord? To obey is better than sacrifice, and to heed is better than the fat of rams'"* (1 Samuel 15:22, NIV).

When we discuss finding common ground, we are really saying to ask the Lord for the area to focus on, what steps to take, and then be obedient. God will advise you on how to handle someone that is being foolish and someone that is being evil. He will also work on your heart and ask you things like, "Do you trust Me?" If our answer is yes, then we will take steps towards obedience.

Ultimately, the goal is to find areas to work ahead so that your family will benefit, your kids will flourish, and you will know without a doubt that God has given you direction, and those steps mean success over what the outcome is.

You Are Responsible for Your Household Only

"Let every person be subject to the governing authorities. For there is no authority except from God, and those that exist have been instituted by God" (Romans 13:1, ESV).

"But I want you to understand that the head of every man is Christ, the head of a wife is her husband, and the head of Christ is God" (1 Corinthians 11:3, ESV).

Instructions for Christian Households

Submit to one another out of reverence for Christ. Wives, submit yourselves to your own husbands as you do to the Lord. For the husband is the head of the wife as Christ is the head of the church, his body, of which he is the Savior. Now as the church submits to Christ, so also wives should submit to their husbands in everything. Husbands, love your wives, just as Christ loved the church and gave himself up for her to make her holy, cleansing her by the washing with water through the word, and to present her to himself as a radiant church, without stain or wrinkle or any other blemish, but holy and blameless. In this same way, husbands ought to love their wives as their own bodies. He who loves his wife loves himself. After all, no one ever hated their own body, but they feed and care for their body, just as Christ does the church— for we are members of his body. "For this reason, a man will leave his father and mother and be united to his wife, and the two will become one flesh." This is a profound mystery—but I am talking about Christ and the church. However, each one of you also must love his wife as he loves himself, and the wife must respect her husband.

Ephesians 5:21–33 (NIV)

Let's break down each of these verses listed above and see how they apply to this chapter on respecting boundaries. The book of Romans states that every person should be under governing authorities. That there is no authority that exists that hasn't been instituted by God. This means when we are divorced, the decree is our authority on how to co-parent and divide time with the kids. The difference is that, once divorced, you no longer fall under the prior authority, which was your husband, or if you are the husband, you no longer are your wife's authority since you are now divorced. As a divorced male, I knew that I was no longer my ex-wife's authority and that I had very limited input, if any, into her household. I could state things I was doing for our daughter in our household, but there was no authority to make her do it. If you are single, you are your own authority in your household, and I would encourage you that get under good spiritual authority so that you don't make unwise decisions. It is biblical to get counsel to help you navigate through the challenges you are going to face.

The second scripture states the head of every man is Christ. The head of a wife is her husband, and the head of Christ is God. In today's culture, this scripture is controversial, but it is still true. Submission is a powerful thing to choose, and as a Christian male/husband/and father, I still choose to submit to my pastor and elders even when I don't like what they decide or tell me. God supernaturally covers me for the decisions I make when I am under authority. It is biblical for a wife to be under her husband's authority, and he should be leading her the way Jesus did for us.

The last part is scripture on a Christian household. This was God's intent. Let's focus on one of the most important parts, though, verse 25. It states, "Husbands, love your wives, just as Christ loved the church and gave himself up for her." The issue with divorce in most cases is that the husband really didn't love his wife the way we are asked. We are not truly willing to give our life for our wife, and that is why the marriage broke. I misled, made poor decisions, and didn't love my first wife like Jesus loved the church. I can say in my second marriage that this has been the example my wife and I have followed, and we have seen blessings because of it. She knows she can trust me because I am spending time with the Lord and listening. She knows that I have godly men who challenge me and will ask me hard questions. She knows she can trust me to lead and sacrifice anything I need to for her as long as I am being obedient to what God is telling me. I know at the end of my life, I will have to give an account for how I lead my family, so I want to do the best I can.

This creates tension, though, in divorce. You no longer have to follow the authority that was originally established, and the water becomes muddy. You want to control things like who they date, who gets to be around your kids, and how your kids are disciplined, but the truth of the matter is you are only responsible for your household. Once you start trying to influence your ex-spouse, then they have the same right to speak into your life.

I am sure you are sitting here and don't really like this section of the book. To be totally vulnerable, it was the hardest thing I have ever walked through. It made me ask things like, "Is God really over everything? Can God cover my children when I am not around or not able to manage what is happening?" It made me ask myself whether I really trust God and who He allows to be in authority.

Take some time and think about things you are still trying to control. Think of areas you need to submit as well to God, spiritual authority, or spouse. Take time to discuss why they have been hard to let go, and you will see that the burden is much lighter this way. You will have to choose trust over control, but in the end, God will prove time and time again that He has a plan, and He will use all this, even when we don't see it or understand it. Our culture is drifting from biblical values, and we need to refocus.

As a divorced man who became a pastor, I have seen that God's Word is the only truth we have. We are not in control of how life works out, but we are in control of choosing Him. We can believe His Word over our feelings, circumstance, or even past hurts because God is sovereign!

I would encourage you to let go and let God. When we take our hands off the wheel and let God direct us, there is something special at that moment. It is when we can feel how much joy, peace, patience, kindness, generosity, faithfulness, gentleness, and self-control He gives us. It is when we let go of control that we start to walk in sanctification, becoming more like Christ.

Chapter Reflection

Holy Spirit, what are You saying to me?

CHAPTER EIGHT:

New Kids, Who Dis?

Do you remember a time you were so excited to get something, and then it was substituted for something different than what you expected? I remember as a kid having generic black and white label cereal, candy, and different canned food in the pantry. It wasn't what I really wanted, but it served the same purpose. The real kicker for me, though, was soda.

I was a huge fan of soda, and I still am. Besides coffee, I drink diet soda. This, of course, is not a book on how to be the healthiest person in the world, so don't judge me. I remember, though, the first time I had diet soda. The issue was no one told me it was diet.

I was at my grandparents' house about to eat lunch when I was asked if I wanted some "pop." I grew up in Pennsylvania, so pop was the common word for soda; living in Texas now, it seems weird to this day when I hear soda referred to as pop. I told them I would love a glass and was even more excited to see how big the cup was my grandfather pulled out. We called him Pop as well but still, I don't know why, just that it was cooler than grandpa. I remember it sitting in front of me, and I was going to try to get a refill as soon as I was done.

I pick up my cup and take a big swig, only to think to myself, *What is this? This is not soda; this is garbage.* It was not sweet, it tasted like chemicals, and I was missing my full sugar binge at this moment. I looked at my family, who all seemed to not notice what was going on, and I asked, "Why does the soda taste so bad?" They were confused till they realized that I had never had diet soda before. It wasn't that it was that bad; it just wasn't what I was expecting! I now drink diet soda only and have gotten used to the taste and fewer calories.

The point of all this is that having a bonus mom or dad is just like diet soda. It doesn't work as a supplement because the kids are used to their birth parents. It takes time to get used to having another adult, to trust them, to know who they are and that they really care. I didn't drink diet soda from that day forward as it was an acquired taste that took time. I had to see that regular soda had a ton of calories and sugar which I know I can over-consume.

The same approach has to be taken by each person as they become a bonus mom and dad. You will have times the kids reject you, challenge you, and try to pin you against their parents; they are kids, and this is what they do. It is an adjustment that they have to face and grow into.

The goal is to be available, as we discussed above when we said give them space. As you grow closer, let them come to you with whatever they need and find ways to connect. Over time the kids will trust you, know you, and your family will be built. God will start working on their hearts, but you must not ever substitute being their parent. I have told my bonus kids that I am not their father but that I am blessed to have them in my life, and I am a better father because of it. I express to them that they have given me a chance to grow and love without trying to supplant their father. This is the best approach we can all take. Avoid being a substitution and allow time to become an addition!

Pray to Love Them as Your Own

The hardest thing about having stepkids is knowing how to love them and treat them right. One part of you wants to treat them the same as yours, but there is an internal struggle that you are not their parent. Your heart is not ready at times to really receive them, and you need God's help to become the parent they need.

It was hard for me to connect at times with each kid, and as we discussed above, I was not trying to be a substitute for their father. I was trying to be an additional supportive authority in their life. I wanted what was best for them, so I prayed for God to show me how to love them. My wife at the time had four kids, and I had one. The youngest was only two when we met, and I couldn't get past the fact that she had a young baby. He wasn't as young as I was imagining and struggling with, but it still made me hesitate and think, *God, can I really take on this many kids?*

I can be selfish at times. I like comfort and nice things. I have had to let the Lord work that out of me, and praying to love stepkids like my own took some big faith steps.

One challenge specifically was using my 401k to pay off some costs we had with the kids. My wife was just finishing school for nursing, I had just taken a job as a pastor, and I knew the Lord was asking me to trust Him financially. We ran into some major bills all of a sudden related to health expenses, education expenses, and housing expenses. I knew there was no other option except to use what I had in my 401k to get us through the year.

New Kids, Who Dis?

At the time, I was very challenged in this because it was money that I had saved over a fifteen-year career. I didn't express my concerns to anyone really but took it to prayer. God was gentle with me but showed me some issues with my heart in this process.

He asked me if my daughter needed it, would I do it? I thought, *Of course*. He said, "Then why don't you love the kids the same way? If they need it, you provide it. You prayed to love them the same as your own." I realized right then that God was using this to show me where my heart was. Was my trust in my bank account, or was it in my family and bonus kids?

God showed me I was hurt in my divorce, so I was hesitant to put that much of my resources into my new family. I was still holding on to pain rather than hope for the future. My pain made me hesitate, and the Lord was healing me by showing me that the family He gave me was just as important as the one I tried to save.

I wish I hadn't hesitated with it. I wish I hadn't questioned God, but years later, I realized that using those funds made me invest in my bonus kids. It made me love them and put my focus on them. I would do anything for them today, and it all started with a prayer to God, asking Him to make my heart bigger and allow my love for them to grow.

If you are struggling to blend your family, maybe it isn't external factors. It might be that you haven't asked the Lord to help you in areas to love and serve your family more. Maybe you still see your kids and their kids as a blended family, but God didn't want that. Just like the church, we are a mixed bag of people who love each other. We serve each other and use family terms such as brothers and sisters. I would suggest you ask the Lord to help you in this area. Ask Him for help to love your stepkids as much as your own and see what He does.

I am blessed to have five awesome kids. I know each one is different, has their own personality, and connects with me individually. I know that we have been through a lot together, but I wouldn't change a thing. God knew what I needed even when I didn't know.

Know Limits and Boundaries

"Do not answer a fool according to his folly, or you yourself will be just like him" (Proverbs 26:4, NIV).

When we are aware of our limits and boundaries, we make better decisions. It allows us to not be foolish and respond to things we shouldn't. Proverbs clearly points out that when we don't have clear limits and boundaries, it is

New Kids, Who Dis?

easy for us to become fools. We will cross boundaries we aren't meant to.

When dealing with boundaries, again, we must ask the Lord for wisdom in this area. My daughter was graduating eighth grade this year, and before the students go to high school, they ask that the parents come to the front and lay hands on their kids to pray over them before they start their next journey in high school. I paused and decided to pray.

I knew that my wife deserved to be up there to pray over my daughter with me and her mom. She has been supportive to my daughter, loving as a mom, and has helped, shaped, and grown her into the awesome kid she is. I paused, though, because two years ago, my wife's daughter had the same thing happen. At that time, though, as I was praying, I heard the Lord say to me, "Don't go up there." This was a time that my stepdaughter had to see her parents support and pray for her, and it was best if I stayed behind. Of course, I wanted to go up, but I knew that I needed to be obedient.

This time as I prayed, the Lord told me to have my wife come up with me. I sent her a text saying to come up and pray at the end when they call the parents. As we walked up and got to my daughter, I saw my ex-wife say hello to Laura, give her a hug, and thank her for being so good to our daughter. It was weird and awesome at the same time. We were the only group up there that had three parents praying over a child and at a Christian school. It made me laugh inside, thinking about what everyone in the crowd was wondering.

My wife then took a picture of our daughter with my ex and me in it. She felt it would be good for Aubrey to have a current photo of her parents on this big day. Ego, pride, and anything else could have stood in the way, but when we humble ourselves and give grace, God does amazing things. We have both healed from past hurts, and our daughter is flourishing because she has three parents that are supportive of her.

Knowing what limits and boundaries to follow only comes from the Holy Spirit. We have to stay connected to the Holy Spirit so that we know what steps to take. I smile because of that day; it showed me my daughter has a great family. It also showed me how thoughtful and loving my wife is to put my daughter ahead of awkwardness, insecurities, or anything else the enemy wanted to use. We didn't give him room that day and, in the end, it was a good celebration!

Chapter Reflection

Holy Spirit, what are You saying to me?

CHAPTER NINE:

It's Not Your Money

"Whoever loves money never has enough; whoever loves wealth is never satisfied with their income. This too is meaningless" (Ecclesiastes 5:10, NIV).

I remember being asked to pay child support. I really was not thrilled about it because I have always taken care of my daughter. In addition, I really didn't understand what my ex-wife's concern was about support, but I decided not to argue. My ex-wife was asking for a very fair amount of support, and it wasn't worth the argument because I knew that I wanted to take care of my daughter. My ex-wife had a great job and the ability to make enough to provide all my daughter needed, but internally, I looked at it differently. I wanted to know without a doubt that I stepped up as a father and provided for my daughter. I knew that if I paid support, no one could ever accuse me of not being a good father. Personally, I wanted to be able to look in the mirror every day and know that even though my daughter was not living here, I still loved and supported her.

I remember thinking about support and the things I paid for, including insurance, phone, and gas to drive back and forth. I was thinking about why this doesn't bother me, and God reminded me of a few things. First, He reminded me that He gave me the ability to make money, and at the same time, He could take it away. We are called to be good stewards of our finances, but it is God who owns it and trust us to do it.

Second, God also reminded me that I was tithing and being generous, which now have become priorities in my life. That is way different than it was before. Scripture states:

> "Bring the whole tithe into the storehouse, that there may be food in my house. Test me in this," says the Lord Almighty, "and see if I will not throw open the floodgates of heaven and pour out so much blessing that there will not be room enough to store it."
>
> **Malachi 3:10 (NIV)**

A common theme I struggled with in my divorce was feeling like I was out of control. This scripture reminded me that I was tithing, paying support, and being generous with my money. It was God's job to pour out blessings that there was not enough room to store them. I want to be very clear, though; the church has misused this passage in the past to mean money. I didn't get rich while doing this; I had blessings such as doors open to do things I never thought possible such as Craig Groeschel complimenting a proposal I wrote and saying it was one of the best he has ever read. The blessing that came through his words encouraged me to take additional faith steps, such as writing this book. God opened doors that were not just financial but were deep desires in my heart. We have to be careful in that area when we discuss finances.

Third, God showed me that I was finally trusting Him with my finances. This allowed me to measure what really matters and that was the impact my giving was creating. I saw people get healing, people getting through hard situations, and most importantly, people giving their life to Jesus. I realized at that moment that the money didn't belong to me; it had always been His. This then allowed me to see I wasn't accountable for what my support paid. I met my obligation when I paid my support; what it was used for is not my issue anymore. It is my ex-wife's responsibility to account to God for those finances.

It is the same reason my wife and I tithe on any child support we get from her ex-husband. I would rather have less money that is fully blessed than a lot that is cursed. When your heart changes and your approach changes, you start to see the benefit of funding things related to the kingdom. You stop trying to control it or justify why you don't do it.

The same goes with tithing to your local church. God doesn't need your money; He wants your heart. He is in control, but the only way we do that is by giving to the church. I have been hurt by pastors who have misused funds that I felt should have been handled better. I have seen fraud in my career as an auditor. The focus we need is our part, to tithe and be generous. The church body is then responsible for what they do with it after I give it. It is no longer my problem. If we can settle that in our hearts, we don't fight giving, paying support, or being obedient when God asks us to give. We build trust with our finances and realize who the true provider is. Maybe your spouse doesn't need the support, maybe they aren't choosing what you want to be done with it; maybe it feels unfair, especially if you didn't want the divorce; but when you see it isn't your money and resources, but we are only stewards of it, you will stop fighting this, and your perspective will change. Be accountable for your part. When I get to heaven, I want to be able to tell the Lord, "Thank You for changing my heart on money and seeing it as a tool rather than a god. Thank You for breaking the love of money off of me. Thank You, God, for allowing me to become a good steward of what You put in my hand and forgive me when I didn't use money the way You intended." This approach will change the dynamic of co-parenting and will alleviate one of the biggest fights that occur. Pray for God to give you wisdom and for the Holy Spirit to change your perspective by changing your heart.

Additional Expenses

Usually, your decree will discuss medical expenses being split. I would highly encourage you, though, to always over-communicate medical decisions and costs. Try to see if it is best for both of you to carry insurance, even if there is an additional cost, so that one party doesn't get blind-sided by the other.

An approach we have taken is that for minor medical expenses, we don't submit every bill to our ex-spouses for copays. We decided that our kids needed counseling, and it would benefit them while growing up. We wanted to pick the counselor and make sure they were Christian to guide our kids on biblical values. Because we made these decisions, we have not sent every bill to our ex-spouse asking for half the copay.

On major medical decisions, we have done this. We try

to communicate what the expense is, why we are deciding to move forward with it, and notify the other parent of the steps and payments due that will need to be split.

The best approach to any of this is that you stick to the decree, have open communication, and if you feel there is additional care you prefer, then don't fight over the expenses. Give your kids what they need, even if it will cost you extra.

Specifically, I remember talking to a divorced friend, and he asked me why I was buying my daughter all her school supplies when I paid support. I knew where they were going but decided to open the box and see what was really going on. I stated that I wanted to bless my daughter, and even though I paid support, my daughter needed to see that I would do more than the minimum. The guy got offended, and I said I was doing more; I carried extra costs that came up with phone, medical, driving, etc. I decided then to ask him a question and flip it around. I asked him, "How will my daughter ever understand that God will give you more than He has to if her own earthly father won't?" I expressed that my heart is that my daughter will know a father's heart, not just that I did what I was required to and paid my support. He admitted I was right and decided that he would do the same with his kids. God doesn't waste anything, and I am glad I was in the position to challenge him only because I was being obedient to what the Holy Spirit told me to do earlier, which was to pay for her school supplies. When we listen to the Holy Spirit, we seem a lot smarter and wiser than we ever are.

The best investment you can make is your legacy. Our kids are our legacy, and it is our job as parents to make sure we equip them the best we can. We are called to be loving parents, and constantly, we will have to fight the urge to push just our agenda, want repayment for minor costs, or get greedy and want more than what is fair.

If you have a parent that isn't paying support or providing medical expenses, I suggest you still take the high road when it comes to discussions. Your kids do not need to know the financial situation or what is going on. They may ask, and you can address their questions, but make sure you reassure them it will work out and that each parent loves them and will do their best to make sure their needs are taken care of. Kids do not need the anxiety, pressure, or negativity that comes when a parent isn't supporting them.

I am not telling you not to address the fact or let it go by. Get an attorney and deal with it but never use your kids to put pressure on the other parent to step up. It isn't fair to them, and it isn't a burden they should ever have to carry.

Who Is the Real Provider?

It still comes down to the overall theme of do you think that our heavenly Father sees you, loves you, and cares for you? Do you trust God to be your provider?

If you are tithing and being generous, then this section of the book isn't directed at you. If you are not, let's take a moment to look at some scriptures and be honest with God if you really trust Him or not, especially with your finances.

In Matthew, Jesus uses a parable to get His point across about what we are to do as believers:

> Then the King will say to those on his right, 'Come, you who are blessed by my Father; take your inheritance, the kingdom prepared for you since the creation of the world. For I was hungry and you gave me something to eat, I was thirsty and you gave me something to drink, I was a stranger and you invited me in, I needed clothes and you clothed me, I was sick and you looked after me, I was in prison and you came to visit me.' Then the righteous will answer him, 'Lord, when did we see you hungry and feed you, or thirsty and give you something to drink? When did we see you a stranger and invite you in, or needing clothes and clothe you? When did we see you sick or in prison and go to

visit you?' The King will reply, 'Truly I tell you, whatever you did for one of the least of these brothers and sisters of mine, you did for me.'

Matthew 25:34–40 (NIV)

I believe this captures many Christians, including me before God changed my heart about money. I would tip God when going to church, give money to a cause if I was guilted, and would think that people need to take care of themselves because I had to work for what I had.

Maybe this is just me, but I see a lot in church where we don't really trust God with finances. God knew that this would be a huge issue for us as believers and put about 2,350 verses related to how we handle money and finances. God is watching what we do with our resources, who we bless with them, and how obedient we are when He asks us to. I had had to choose between paying a late fee on a bill or tithing, and let me tell you, the best miracles I have seen are when I was struggling but gave when God told me. Money lasted longer, people took us on date nights when we didn't have a dime in the bank, and food would be given to us. This happened time and time again, and I know that people did it out of love for the Lord.

As Jesus talks about in this parable, He wants us to help those who are struggling. If you have a single parent in your church, take them to dinner; if you have a couple that is remarried, spend time with them and love on them; if you have kids that come from split households, encourage them that they have families that love them.

When we do this, our heavenly Father looks down and smiles. He sees that we have His heart. God doesn't need your finances, but He does want to use you. Think of the issues we could solve if we put our own desires, greed, and selfish ambition behind us and gave. Not because we have to, but because we want to.

As I write this book, I can share that half of it was paid for by people who believed that the church needed to address this topic. They believe having a resource like this would allow us to address what biblical divorce is, what repentance looks like if you aren't biblically divorced, which doesn't mean reconciliation, and that we can guide people to co-parent well and build a better foundation for kids who come from broken homes. They believed it would be a tool that would bless many families, and I am honored that God put it in their hearts.

This is what I meant earlier when I said God opened the floodgates. He allowed a childhood dream of mine to become a reality. Writing has been buried deep in my heart for some time now, and I am humbled by what our God can do. It wasn't an easy road, but through these challenges, He built a story that I hope will help you see His goodness.

Chapter Reflection

Holy Spirit, what are You saying to me?

CHAPTER TEN:

Changing Residence

In most cases, parents want time with their children. Changing residences once it has been established will cause a lot of stress, pressure, and struggles with your feelings. There are two ways kids request to change residence. The first is that they live with the other parent and want to move in with you. The second way they move is that they live with you and want to move in with another parent. One seems better and easier than the other, but hopefully, this chapter and our experience will help guide you when your child requests to move in or out.

Please hear this, though, when a child asks to move in or move out, do not put guilt, shame, or condemnation on them. If you care about the relationship, discuss your issues with a counselor or spiritual authority rather than the child who is requesting it. I am not saying you can't have discussions on why the child wants to move, but do not make them feel guilty for wanting to discuss it like it is wrong to have an open conversation with them about it. If it really isn't safe for the child to change residence, ask them to trust your decision-making and express that your concern is always that they are in the best environment. Ask them to trust you to make hard decisions when their safety is at risk. However, if it is just because you don't like your ex-spouse, don't want them in a different environment, etc., then you will have to pray for the Holy Spirit to guide you and see if that is a battle you are willing to have.

In our case, the Lord was very clear not to fight the kids when they requested to move. We had discussions instead and made sure they were okay with their decisions. As my wife and I have been married, we had to allow two of our kids to live with another parent. We also had one that requested to live with us. I have been on both ends, and each time we have discussed it, we have tried to focus on facts rather than feelings, and we stayed open to changing schools and schedules and honoring their request if we didn't have biblical reasons not to allow them to move. Scripture states, *"Parents, don't come down too hard on your children or you'll crush their spirits"* (Colossians 3:21, MSG).

It is important you always move forward with guid-

Changing Residence

ance from the Holy Spirit and keep the relationship with your child at the forefront. This might mean letting go and allowing them an opportunity to move even if you don't like it or agree with it. The key is creating an environment where the child knows they are loved, that your door is always open as long as they will submit to your rules and authority, and that you want what is best for them. You give them what they need, not just what they want. When you approach it this way, it will cause some internal struggles that you will have to process through, but in the end, you will always have your door open to keep a relationship far beyond their early years when they need a parent. One day they will be adults, and they will ask you some hard questions; make sure you are guided by the Holy Spirit to ensure that you can stand on them and explain them at a later date.

I always want our kids to know that we are open to them living with either parent. When walking through these situations, we stated that. We also clarified that they would not switch between households when deciding this and get parents pinned against each other. We discussed with the other parent that if this happens, the child was committing to at least two years living elsewhere even though the court only required a year. We wanted the child to have stability and not just go to whatever house had rules that fit that moment in their life. Teens are tricky, so we eliminated some of the hurdles we thought we would see if we didn't clearly lay out those boundaries.

When Kids Ask to Move

I remember driving one day when my daughter was talking about moving in with us. She said that she was praying and felt that when she was in seventh grade, she would come to the private Christian school in our area. I was excited, happy to know the Lord was putting that in her heart, and to be honest, she was going into sixth grade, and I was ready for her to transfer now.

I paused, though, and held back my reaction. I asked her if she was able to discuss it with her mom or if she was just bringing this up to me. She shared that it had been in her heart, but she was nervous to say anything because of how it might be taken. It was a mature observation for a sixth-grader, and I knew that she needed some guidance rather than persuasion. I suggested that she focus on the start of school for now. I also told her to start praying and looking for the opportunity to share with her mom what she had in her heart.

I expressed that it was clearly her decision, but I was

not going to push it or interfere. "If this was something you felt God put in your heart, then you need to take a faith step and discuss it with your mom when the opportunity comes." She listened and looked disappointed because I was not going to lead the conversation. I felt if the Lord was putting it in her heart, then He would put it in her mom's heart as well.

After a few months, my ex-wife asked if we could talk. It was the start of COVID, and my daughter was being homeschooled and staying with us because I was working each day remotely. I said sure and knew, based on my daughter's conversation with me, that she had talked to her mom. My ex-wife asked if my wife and I could come to the area and have dinner with her and her boyfriend. We agreed and sat and discussed what the move, school, and terms would be in the new decree. This was great because I was able to send that to my attorney, and within a few months, we had a new agreement.

My daughter has flourished, and it built trust between her mom and her to have those hard conversations. Her mom has been supportive and encouraged her as she has done well here in her new environment. My ex-wife has never put pressure on our daughter, and it has been such a healing process for all of us. I am encouraged by it and thankful that we have her here. We always agree to give extra time when we can to her mom, and her mom has been just as flexible with us. This is what happens when you take steps to let go of your right to be right and approach it the way God intends.

When Kids Ask to Move With Other Parent

My wife and I were definitely getting into the teenage years when her daughter asked to move in with her father. If I am being transparent, it didn't excite me to have any of our kids not wanting to live with us most of the time.

We asked our daughter if she was sure about it. We asked if she was good with changing schools and living in a new area and had the same discussion we had with my daughter when she moved here. We expressed that our door is always open, but when she decides this, she will stick with her decision for quite some time. She agreed, and we used our attorney to negotiate a modification to the decree.

In both these situations, we had to really hide our feelings. In one, we were happy; in the other, we were sad and concerned. My wife and I talked together, but we never wanted to interfere with the decisions our kids were making. During these times, the Holy Spirit said the same thing over and over, which was, "Do you trust Me?" We felt God asking us time and time again if we trusted Him no matter what the circumstances, and the answer was always the same. Kids are a temporary assignment, and we need to trust the Lord with them. They will grow up, move out, maybe get married, and leave and cleave. No matter what, we know that our kids belong to the Lord.

Moving with Kids After Divorce

When we got married, we bought my in-laws' house. It was a big, old house that allowed each kid to have plenty of space. I liked the house but bought it because I felt the Lord showed me a few things. He showed me our kids had transitioned enough, and they were familiar with the house since my wife's parents owned it. The house was also in our budget. The house was older and really, really, really big. It took forever to clean because it was about 4,800 square feet.

I was getting tired of cleaning and taking care of it and felt it was time to downsize but upgrade to a newer home. My wife and I prayed about it, and we had enough equity to make the move a reality. We didn't move out of the same city, but it was across town. The kids go to a private school, so that didn't impact them; however, that didn't mean the move didn't affect them.

Some of the kids were so excited because the new house meant new furniture. They were excited to be in a neighborhood where we would allow them to ride their bikes anywhere in it, partially because they are older now. They were pumped to be close to the mall and different restaurants and friends that were close.

Some of the other kids, though, were not that excited. They were used to the house we were in. They were leaving friends that lived close by that they could walk to their house anytime they wanted. They were disappointed that the house was actually going to be owned by another family.

We let the kids react how they needed to as long as they stayed respectful. If they showed honor, their opinion would be heard, but it didn't guarantee input into our decision-making. Laura and I are a team, and we would do what we felt were the right steps for our family. We made sure not to show the new house to the kids as well until the contract was executed because they had so much transition.

Changing Residence

During the move, we let each kid have space when they needed it and would check in on them. We didn't take negative or positive comments personally; we just gave them time to adjust. After being in the house now for a few months, each kid is loving it and thriving. They don't hold on to the past because they are finding good memories in this house as well.

When moving, give your kids time to embrace their feelings and even some past hurts. Do not take it personally and allow them time to process. This will ensure they feel heard and loved. It also will allow them to be open to the new location and home quicker than just shutting them down or not listening.

Chapter Reflection

Holy Spirit, what are You saying to me?

CHAPTER ELEVEN:

Changing Your Legacy Through Forgiveness

Then Peter came to Jesus and asked, "Lord, how many times may my brother sin against me and I forgive him, up to seven times?" Jesus said to him, "I tell you, not seven times but seventy times seven! "The holy nation of heaven is like a king who wanted to find out how much money his servants owed him. As he began, one of the servants was brought to him who owed him very much money. He could pay nothing that he owed. So the king spoke the word that he and his wife and his children and all that he had should be sold to pay what he owed. The servant got down on his face in front of the king. He said, 'Give me time, and I will pay you all the money.' Then the king took pity on his servant and let him go. He told him he did not have to pay the money back. "But that servant went out and found one of the other servants who owed him very little money. He took hold of his neck and said, 'Pay me the money you owe me!' The other servant got down at his feet and said, 'Give me time, and I will pay you all the money.' But he would not. He had him put in prison until he could pay the money. "When his other servants saw what had happened, they were very sorry. They came and told the king all that was done. Then the king called for the first one. He said, 'You bad servant! I forgave you. I said that you would not have to pay back any of the money you owed me because you asked me. Should you not have had pity on the other servant, even as I had pity on you?' The king was very angry. He handed him over to men who would beat and hurt him until he paid all the money he owed. So will My Father in heaven do to you, if each one of you does not forgive his brother from his heart."

Matthew 18:21–35 (NLV)

Forgiveness is not an easy thing to do, whether it is forgiving yourself, your ex-spouse, or anyone that might have hurt you in the divorce process. However, when I read these verses above, we are taught two very important lessons by Jesus. First is that we constantly should be forgiving anyone that has wronged us. Forgiveness doesn't mean eliminating boundaries, having restoration, or acting like it didn't happen. Forgiveness is giving grace for what did happen and realizing that it was wrong but not continuing to hold it against someone. The second thing Jesus points out in this parable is that if we don't forgive, we will be punished and tortured till we repay our debt.

Because Jesus died on the cross, we don't have to repay our debt; He paid it for us. Jesus knew your sin from past, present, and future and still laid down His life so you can have forgiveness. This is what God is asking you right now. Biblical divorce comes through adultery and abandonment; however, even when it isn't biblical, but you repented from it, then there is forgiveness that must occur.

You have to forgive the other person. Believe it or not, this is easier than the next person you have to forgive. Remember that Jesus died for them too. They are a soul that God loves and has a plan for. Just to reiterate, though, if you forgive the person who hurt you and left you, that doesn't mean that you need to return to the pain or have restoration in your prior marriage. There were real scars, and I am not downplaying them. But it is important you don't carry them. Jesus' parable is showing us that we are not responsible for passing judgment or punishment; that is God's job, not ours, so let Him handle it. Our job is to forgive so that we can walk in freedom.

The next person you need to forgive is yourself. You made mistakes, too, as we all do in life. This is way harder, at least for me, because I don't really like admitting how I added to the situation, and it's hard to forgive things that I chose. I made the decision to have a pornography issue in my first marriage, I made the decision to not love my wife like Jesus loved the church, and I made the decision to put my daughter ahead of my ex-wife while we were married. These decisions caused a lot of pain, and I was responsible for them. Luckily God's grace applies to you, too, not just your ex. I had to work through forgiving myself for misleading, letting boundaries slide, and not leading biblically. I had to work through like myself again after the divorce, and it was all while I was on the other side of failure. Don't get caught in blame; instead, focus on forgiveness.

Building a Strong Foundation

One thing Christians can mess up is thinking that the goal of this journey is to be married and have kids. I thought for many years the American dream was gospel. I believed that if I achieved a great job, marriage, kids, and a nice house, then God really loved me, and I was walking in obedience. That is not in Scripture, but prosperity gospel, and our culture have made it that way. God's plan for you may not call you to get married again. Paul said it is better for some of us not to be married.

However, if you are called to remarriage, understand it must be built on a strong foundation. Scripture states,

> Two are better than one, because they have a good return for their labor: If either of them falls down, one can help the other up. But pity anyone who falls and has no one to help them up. Also, if two lie down together, they will keep warm. But how can one keep warm alone? Though one may be overpowered, two can defend themselves. A cord of three strands is not quickly broken.
>
> **Ecclesiastes 4:9–12 (NIV)**

It is good to be married, and God may have called you to remarriage; however, without God being in the center, it will not sustain itself. I would recommend that you pray for your spouse if you aren't remarried yet. If you are, then pray with your spouse daily out loud. It may not be comfortable or something you have done before, but it helps keep God in the center of your relationship. Gallup poll showed that couples who pray together face a divorce rate of 1 out of 1,153 marriages. That means your marriage is likely to succeed if you pray together out loud. I would suggest, in addition to praying out loud, that you read your

Bible daily, serve in the local church together, and build time into the day to discuss what God is asking you. It will take faith steps, but the best thing you can give your kids after a divorce is a healthy marriage to model after. In reality, we all need more healthy marriages modeled in society, and the key is to have God in the middle of it.

Share Your Story

"'Return home and tell how much God has done for you.' So the man went away and told all over town how much Jesus had done for him" (Luke 8:39, NIV).

Jesus tells a man to go home and share what He has done for him. This came after Jesus cast out demons into pigs and then drowned them. This miracle is one of my favorites because it applies to the demons I let in my life. God has removed my addiction to pornography and pain pills, removed my pride, and changed my life. When you read this book, it is scary to put words on paper and open up about the shortfalls I have had.

God knows I am far from perfect and that our family is still blending. God knows that my wife and I can disagree on things, but He keeps us covered as we navigate life after a divorce. God has carried us through the good times and the bad, but in the end, the only thing I have is Him. He has never failed me, never forgotten me, and never left me. God is my anchor, and my goal in writing this was to share my story. Now that I shared my story, I am going to ask you to do something for me. Find people who need your help. Don't let pride get in the way; share your failures with them as well. Share of the times that you were lost, scared, hurt, fearful, and didn't have enough but knew that God carried you through.

Our story is the most critical tool God gave us. Whether you believe what I have shared or not, it is my story. No one can argue with me about what God has done for me in my life. He wants to do the same for you. God has a purpose for you, but it takes being in a relationship with Jesus. Maybe you have gotten away from the Lord in this time; my hope is that you will repent. My hope is that if you didn't have a true relationship with God or did and walked away from it, you will pray this simple prayer. You can say it out loud or in your heart; it doesn't matter. If you want to come back to the Lord, just say it with me, friend:

Jesus, I believe You are the Son of God. I believe You died on the cross for the forgiveness of my sin's past, present, and future. I invite You into my heart. Lead me and guide me; I don't want to live my life my way anymore.

Thank You, Jesus, for saving me. Amen.

If you prayed that, congratulations! Your life is about to change. If you found stories in this book helpful, please share it or give a copy to someone who is walking through a divorce, co-parenting, single, or remarried again.

Most importantly, share with people what God has done through your challenges and pain. Share your mistakes and allow your story to impact others. It is the most powerful tool you have besides the Word of God, so use it.

God bless,

Doug Case.

Chapter Reflection

Holy Spirit, what are You saying to me?

Appendix

Please feel free to use this as a tool and guideline. The purpose of this is not to be rules and regulations but a guide to help your family establish clear expectations.

Family Constitution

Privileges and Responsibilities

As your parents, one of our biggest jobs is to help you grow into who God designed you to be. We give you responsibilities (jobs) and privileges (freedoms) based on your maturity. The more you grow, the more responsibilities you are trusted with and, therefore, the more freedom you have! Until one day when you are fully mature, responsible, and trustworthy enough to go out on your own and enjoy all of life's responsibilities and privileges!

Our Desire for You

Our desire for you, our children, is that you will each grow up to be healthy, loving, productive people who are happy and fulfilled by doing what God has called each of you to do. When we see behaviors and attitudes that don't line up with what we see the finished product to be, it is our duty to help you change that.

We want each of you to love God, love people, and work hard at what God has called you to. We love you all so much and want God's best for you!

Light System

To help us all get on the same page regarding what is expected of you, we are going to implement the *light system*. The system will include three places that you may find yourself on any day. Green, yellow, or red.

You will start each day in green. It is your choice to move to yellow or red. To stay in green for the day, your responsibilities have to be taken care of by you. When you do what is expected, you stay in green! When you stay in green, you get to enjoy all the freedoms and privileges of

Appendix

being in green.

When you decide to break the agreements we have made and not fulfill your responsibilities, then you will be placed in yellow or red according to how you decided to break your agreement.

You will have an opportunity to move back to green each time you struggle or go against what you have agreed to do. So instead of us pulling privileges away for days on end, you will have a chance each day to make it right. How long you are in yellow or red is up to us, but we are looking for your attitudes to change and your heart to be willing to do the right thing when given a chance.

The details of what kid has which responsibilities are below. These include personal chores, joint chores, managing yourself, and schoolwork.

Green: all responsibilities are fulfilled with excellence.

- [ ] Personal responsibilities.
- [ ] Behavior/Attitude.
- [ ] Individual chores.
- [ ] Schoolwork.

Yellow: partially or not responsible in one or more areas (we have to remind or correct).

- ☐ No electronics.
- ☐ Complete or correct the irresponsibility.
- ☐ Up to one-hour trial period or additional chores.

Red: willfully irresponsible (direct disobedience, unrepentant, any instance of violence, temper, lying).

- ☐ Room alone for up to three hours or additional chores.
- ☐ Write an apology letter.

Expectations

Behavior/Attitude

Love—God and people.

Respect—others' feelings, wishes, and rights.

Listen—take turns in discussion and pay attention.

Self-Control—manage your actions, feelings, and emotions.

Patience—accept changes without getting angry or upset.

Grace—give freely of love and favor even if the other person doesn't deserve it.

Personal Responsibilities

Bedtime

School year—8:30 p.m./9 p.m.

Summer—9 p.m./9:30 p.m.

Mornings

School—7 a.m. weekdays/10:30 a.m. Saturday.

Summer—9 a.m. weekdays/10:30 a.m. Saturday.

Hygiene

Teeth brushed twice a day, bath/shower daily.

Three meals and one snack—anything else must be requested.

Laundry—dirty in baskets, clean folded and put away.

Dishes—put in the sink after meals.

Clean up after group playtime—Legos, outside games, etc.

Rooms—All

Bed made daily.

Room picked up daily—cups put away daily, no food ever allowed.

Trash is in a can and emptied once a week into big trash.

Floors vacuumed weekly.

Closet cleaned and organized once a week.

Bathrooms—All

Counter cleared daily—toiletries put away.

Weekly wipe down: included counters, toilets, shower/tub.

Weekly sweep and mop.

Appendix

Laundry—All

Put dirty clothes in the hallway basket.

Clean your own laundry.

Everybody folds towels.

Baskets in the living room.

Fold and put away.

Individual Chores

Living Room—Child 5

Before electronics and after dinner:

Pillows on couches.

Blankets in the basket.

Controllers put away.

Dog toys in the dog bed.

Countertops + Table—Child 4

Wipe down after each meal with a paper towel and disinfectant or Clorox wipe.

Floors—Child 1 and Child 2

Sweep:

Kitchen and dining room after lunch and after dinner.

Hallways twice a week.

Living room, foyer twice a week.

Mop:

Kitchen, dining, hallways, and living room weekly.

Trash—Child 3

When full, take out to can.

Put a new liner in.

Recycling to can before shower.

Cans to the road Monday night.

Empty cans brought in by Tuesday night.

Dog Poop—Child 3

Front and back yard three times a week.

Appendix

Dishes—Child 1 and Child 2

Empty sink after lunch and after dinner.

Put away hand-dried dishes nightly.

Run load nightly.

Empty clean dishes each morning.

Dogs

Potty before play.

Bathed weekly—Child 2.

Fed nightly after showers—Child 3.

Water bowl checked at breakfast/lunch/dinner—Child 3.

CPSIA information can be obtained
at www.ICGtesting.com
Printed in the USA
LVHW012056101022
730380LV00013B/501